D1232068

POLITICAL MURDER
IN CENTRAL
AMERICA

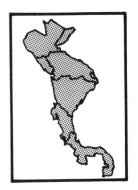

Death Squads & U.S. Policies

Gary E. McCuen

IDEAS IN CONFLICT SERIES

publications inc.
411 Mallalieu Drive
Hudson, Wisconsin 54016

Illustration & photo credits
Carol & Simpson 12, 59, 64, 108, Christic Institute 97, Granma 112, Guardian 26, 88, Ollie Harrington 19, 123, Charles Keller, 33, Medical Aid for El Salvador Fund 75, The Militant 71, The Minneapolis Star & Tribune 60, Nicaragua Solidarity Committee 119, Oxfam America 48, 81, 94, 104, USA Today 98, Washington Post Writers Group 42, 57

©1985 by Gary E. McCuen Publications, Inc.

publications inc.

411 Mallalieu Drive ● Hudson, Wisconsin 54016 ●
(715) 386-5662
International Standard Book Number 0-86596-050-X
Printed in the United States of America

CONTENTS

READINGS

READINGS

REASONING SKILL DEVELOPMENT

*These activities may be used as individualized study
guides for students in libraries and resource centers or as
discussion catalysts in small group and classroom
discussions.*

IDEAS in CONFLICT ®

This series features ideas in conflict on political, social and moral issues. It presents counterpoints, debates, opinions, commentary and analysis for use in libraries and classrooms. Each title in the series uses one or more of the following basic elements:

Introductions that present an issue overview giving historic background and/or a description of the controversy.

Counterpoints and debates carefully chosen from publications, books, and position papers on the political right and left to help librarians and teachers respond to requests that treatment of public issues be fair and balanced.

Symposiums and forums that go beyond debates that can polarize and oversimplify. These present commentary from across the political spectrum that reflect how complex issues attract many shades of opinion.

A global emphasis with foreign perspectives and surveys on various moral questions and political issues that will help readers to place subject matter in a less culture-bound and ethno-centric frame of reference. In an ever shrinking and interdependent world, understanding and cooperation are essential. Many issues are global in nature and can· be effectively dealt with only by common efforts and international understanding.

Reasoning skill study guides and discussion activities provide ready made tools for helping with critical reading and evaluation of content. The guides and activities deal with one or more of the following:

RECOGNIZING AUTHOR'S POINT OF VIEW

INTERPRETING EDITORIAL CARTOONS

VALUES IN CONFLICT

WHAT IS EDITORIAL BIAS?

WHAT IS SEX BIAS?

WHAT IS POLITICAL BIAS?

WHAT IS ETHNOCENTRIC BIAS?

WHAT IS RACE BIAS?

WHAT IS RELIGIOUS BIAS?

From across **the political spectrum** varied sources are pre-sented for research projects and classroom discussions. Diverse opinions in the series come from magazines, newspapers, syndi-cated columnists, books, political speeches, foreign nations, and position papers by corporations and non-profit institutions.

About The Editor

Gary E. McCuen is an author and publisher of anthologies for public libraries and curriculum materials for schools. Over the past 14 years his publications of over 200 titles have specialized in social, moral and political conflict. They include books, pamphlets, cassettes, tabloids, filmstrips and simulation games, many of them designed from his curriculums during 11 years of teaching junior and senior high school social studies. At present he is the editor and publisher of the *Ideas in Conflict* series and the *Editorial Forum* series.

INTRODUCTION

The statistics are simply astounding. Over 40,000 political murders in El Salvador and 30,000 in Guatemala have been reported in press releases. Estimates place over 120,000 Salvadoran refugees and 100,000 Guatemalan refugees in Mexico, over 300,000 Salvadoran and Guatemalan refugees in the United States and thousands more displaced within El Salvador, Guatemala and Nicaragua.

Stories of massive human rights violations stagger the imagination. The torture of parents in front of their children and children in front of their parents are related by human rights organizations. They report the establishment of institutions that process thousands of children and adults through torture centers before they are killed by one gruesome manner or another. Press reports daily carry testimony from survivors telling of slayings of pregnant women, cutting out of fetuses, raping of young girls, throat-cutting and beheadings.

Chapters one and two present *ideas in conflict* on the political violence from the Central American right and left. Other chapters present counterpoints on death squads and U.S. policy, a debate on the questions of sanctuary for Central American refugees in the United States and foreign perspectives on the Central American conflicts.

CHAPTER 1

TERROR ON THE RIGHT: RIGHT-WING VIOLENCE IN CENTRAL AMERICA

TERROR ON THE RIGHT

NO ONE IS SAFE

Aryeh Neier

Aryeh Neier is Vice Chairman of America's Watch, an international organization concerned with human rights violations. Over the past few years more than a dozen of the America's Watch executive committee and staff have travelled to Central America to gather information on the human rights situation. They have interviewed heads of government, military commanders, police chiefs, prisoners, rank and file soldiers, priests, journalists, lawyers, judges, doctors, refugee workers and victims of human rights abuses and members of their families.

Points to Consider

1. What has been the extent of violence in El Salvador?
2. Who commits this violence and why does it take place?
3. How should the U.S. respond to the human rights abuses in El Salvador?
4. How is information on the political killings obtained?

Excerpted from testimony presented by Aryeh Neier before the National Bipartisan Commission on Central America, 1984. Henry Kissinger was the chairman of this committee.

"Well, there goes another bleeding-heart liberal!"

Murders of civilian non-combatants

Since October 1979, human rights organizations affiliated with the Roman Catholic Archdiocese of San Salvador (until May 1982, Socorro Juridico; since May 1982, Tutela Legal) have tabulated more than 37,000 murders of civilian non-combatants by government security forces and by paramilitary forces allied with them. In the past year, political murders of civilian non-combatants tabulated by Tutela Legal have continued at the rate of about a hundred a week—an astonishing number any place and all the more horrifying given the tiny population of El Salvador and the fact that the security forces should be running out of politically suspect persons to murder.

In January 1983, Tutela Legal tabulated 430 murders of civilian non-combatants by government security forces and by paramilitary forces allied with them; in February 1983, Tutela Legal tabulated 537 such murders; in March 1983, 329 such murders; in April 1983, 386 such murders; in May 1983, 503 such murders; in June 1983, 342 such murders; in July 1983, 424 such murders; in August 1983, 318 such murders.

No One Is Safe

Early morning in El Salvador. The village of San Jose is still asleep. Its peaceful silence is broken by the sound of heavy trucks and jeeps pulling into the center of the canton.

It is the National Guard. Troops pour from the vehicles, surrounding each house. Bull horns announce that the tiny hamlet is to be searched for rebels and weapons.

The soldiers tear apart the houses, destroying furniture, shooting livestock, tearing up gardens, pocketing money and other valuables. They throw clothing and bedding out into the street, piling them in mounds and setting them on fire. The air is black with smoke.

A little girl is crying . . . "They're burning my dress. They're burning my dress."

Nine villagers, one a fifteen year old boy, are herded into one of the houses. Their thumbs are tied behind their backs. Acid is thrown into each face. Their screams are terrifying.

Then *they are marched through the smoke, through the tears, through the screams of their mothers and wives to a place just outside the village where the soldiers execute them with machetes.*

The next day grieving villagers attempt to bury their dead. But the soldiers return and drive them away . . . The people of San Jose become additional homeless numbers, joining thousands in El Salvador who are displaced persons . . . refugees . . . in their own country.

No one is safe . . . not children, not mothers, not teachers or field workers, not ministers or priests or nuns . . . even an archbishop has fallen victim to an assassin's bullet.

More than 30,000 people have been killed in El Salvador over the past three years.

Excerpted from an Oxfam America public position paper, 1984.

All told, therefore, during the first eight months of 1983, the Archdiocese of San Salvador recorded 3,269 murders of civilian non-combatants by the security forces of the government of El Salvador and paramilitary forces allied with them. For purposes of comparison, the number of such murders recorded by the Archdiocese during the previous eight months—that is, May 1, 1982 through December 31, 1982—was 3,070. Accordingly, the number of recorded murders of non-combatants is rising.

It should be noted, of course, that the number of murders that the Archdiocese records understates the total. The Archdiocese has difficulty obtaining information on political murders in parts of the country remote from San Salvador because it insists on obtaining first-hand testimony from witnesses or family members if a murder is to be included in its tabulations . . .

Human rights disaster

El Salvador is a human rights disaster area. There is no prospect of significant improvement. Though the United States has made strenuous efforts to persuade the security forces to curtail human rights abuses, these efforts—even in such matters as the murder of U.S. citizens—have been unavailing. The Salvadoran security forces are confident that U.S. support will continue, no matter what. Accordingly, they are not moved by U.S. strictures about human rights abuses.

The Salvadoran government's authority derives mainly from its practice of terror. This seems the only explanation for the continuing enormous rate of political murders and disappearances by its security forces. By now, those forces should be running out of politically suspect persons to kill. They keep killing, however, to maintain the terror.

It is nonsense to assert, as the Department of State does frequently, that El Salvador is undergoing a process of democratic development. Democracy implies choice and, plainly, the security forces will not tolerate certain choices. Accordingly, they have murdered or driven into exile the political leadership of the left and some of the political leadership of the center. Other principal targets for murder include those who advocate negotiations with the left and those who themselves denounce political murders. Religious leaders, human rights workers, refugee and relief workers, union leaders, teachers, journalists and doctors have also all been special targets of political murders and disappearances. A sufficient number of such persons have been killed so that, in a tiny impoverished country such as El Salvador, it may well be that the possibilities for democracy have been eradicated for the foreseeable future . . .

They Made Me Watch

The soldiers asked if I was his mother, and I said I was. And they asked if I knew that he had been going into the hills to join the guerrillas, and I said that he never went to the hills, that it must be a mistake. But they laughed and they said no, it was no mistake, and that a mother is always the last to know her own children.

They said that they would show me what kind of a son I had. And they made me come with them to a big barn in the middle of the country. They made me watch everything. They made me watch when they tied his thumbs behind him with barbed wire and made the wire tighter and tighter until his thumbs turned purple. They made me watch when they put a rope through his hands tied like that, threw the other end of the rope over the rafters, and then lifted him up and let him hang there, slowly turning, with all the weight of his body hanging from his blue thumbs. And they made me watch when they tore his clothes off and tied a bucket to his genitals, and every half an hour they'd come back and into the bucket they would put one more small stone.

I begged and begged them to let me die in his place, but they said nothing. They were like men who were bored by all of this. Like it was something so common, all this suffering and screaming. You know how long it took my Jaimie to die? Sixteen hours. Sixteen hours I was there and my son was so close. There was nothing I could do for him, nothing—not even dying would have helped.

Interview of Salvadoran Mother, *The Progressive*, March, 1983, p. 43.

Accordingly, the choice for the United States is to continue to sponsor the security forces, in full knowledge of their murderousness, or to end military support for El Salvador and seek other means to protect those security interests the United States may have in the region. The option of providing massive military support while trying to promote reforms is no option at all. It has been tried for more than three years and there is not the smallest sign of headway.

THE TERROR AND TORTURE CONTINUE

National Labor Committee

The following statement was made on the basis of a fact-finding trip to El Salvador by a delegation of the National Labor Committee in Support of Democracy and Human Rights in El Salvador. The National Labor Committee is chaired by Douglas Fraser, former president of the United Auto Workers; Jack Sheinkman, secretary-treasurer of the Amalgamated Clothing and Textile Workers; and William Winpisinger, president of the International Association of Machinists.

Points To Consider

1. How is the daily terror in El Salvador described?
2. What were the refugee camps like?
3. How was torture used?
4. What recommendation is made for future U.S. policy and military aid?

Excerpted from a report by the National Labor Committee, 1983.

17

The daily terror of El Salvadoran life continues unabated. To exercise democratic rights, to speak out in opposition to the government, remains the equivalent of signing your own death warrant.

At a refugee camp, we spoke with two dozen released political prisoners living and hiding in a makeshift shack. They were there, they told us, because it was not safe for released political prisoners to be out openly on the streets. They felt very strongly that as released political prisoners they were still "subversives"—and thus targets—in the eyes of the El Salvadoran security forces and allied death squads.

One released prisoner, they told us, had already been "disappeared." She was pregnant and had gone back home to her village after her release. She eventually turned up dead, with her fetus lying dead on her chest.

We did not see this corpse. We have no proof that this murder of a released political prisoner actually happened as described to us. But we do know that the political prisoners hiding in that shack believed that incident to be true and feared for their own lives. They told us that they wouldn't leave their shack until plans had been set up to spirit them out of the country . . . **There is no sense of freedom in the Salvadoran political atmosphere.**

The daily terror of El Salvadoran life continues unabated. To exercise democratic rights, to speak out in opposition to the government, remains the equivalent of signing your own death warrant. We met with the Mothers of the Disappeared, a group that keeps the gruesome tally of the missing. The Mothers of the Disappeared report 96 recent kidnappings, of which 94 were by the right.

One respected source of independent data within El Salvador, the legal aid office of the Archdiocese of San Salvador (Tutela Legal), told us that there have been 1,500 reported political assassinations in the first four months of 1983, mostly around urban areas.

In the rural areas, the Christian base communities have ceased to exist in many areas controlled by the government. The Christian lay communities have been a key element in the political awakening of the Salvadoran peasantry—and a prime target for the right-wing death squads.

We spoke to a rural priest who described what has happened: "They started by frightening the lay preachers. Then they started

18

"Nope, nobody in there is interested in no kind'a body count from Central America but if y'all could produce somep'n from Poland . . ."

killing the lay preachers. Then they started killing whoever was available. You can barely find Christian communities in rural areas today because people are afraid to get together."

In San Salvador, we visited the city's largest refugee camp, a church-protected sanctuary for 1,200 peasants driven from their homes over two years ago by a government military offensive against the guerrilla forces who had established a presence in the peasants' home provinces. Nearly every family in the refu-

Over 40,000 Slaughtered

Today, church-based Salvadoran human rights groups report that almost 40,000 people have been systematically slaughtered by government "security" forces—*using U.S. guns and ammunition*—since 1979. Thousands more have been killed in Guatemala. Astonishingly, this hemisphere's worst human rights violators—who *routinely* terrorize, murder, torture, and abduct their own citizens—were recently "certified" as having made "concerted and significant" progress toward protecting people's lives, in a cynical ploy by the Reagan Administration to "qualify" El Salvador for increased U.S. aid.

Martin Sheen, War Resisters League, 1983

gee camp had had a family member killed, belongings taken, homes burned. None of the refugees we saw had identity papers—or had left the camp since they entered it. They now fear Death Squad violence should they venture outside the camp gates.

We agree wholeheartedly with the candid appraisal of current Salvadoran reality that we received from the U.S. Embassy's deputy chief of mission, Kenneth Bleakley. El Salvador, he told us, is in a "sick situation".

"There can be no guarantees of anybody's safety," Bleakley told us plainly.

In this atmosphere, the U.S. government presses for elections that few in El Salvador want . . .

In El Salvador, the official use of torture continues.

On our first night in El Salvador, a veteran U.S. journalist set the Salvadoran mood for us.

"Death is not the problem here," he said. "It's the terror—heads lying in the street, genitals stuffed in mouths, dead chickens up vaginas."

Virtually all the current or former political prisoners we spoke with had been tortured. We spoke to victims of beatings, electric shock, suffocation, and sleep deprivation. The torture inevitably came at the hands of internal security forces, often in private residences.

We spoke with a Lutheran doctor at Mariona Prison who had

had so much electric shock applied to his arms that he thought his shoulder had been dislocated. A bag had also been placed over the doctor's head, filled with a calcium chemical, and drawn around his neck repeatedly until the doctor had lost consciousness.

The chief of El Salvador's National Police, Col. Reynaldo López Nuila, also sits on the government's new Human Rights Commission. The colonel told us that he took exception to the physical interrogation methods of the Treasury Police, another arm of the Salvadoran security forces. His department, the colonel explained, preferred sleep deprivation and other "psychological" methods to the more brutal physical techniques practiced by the Treasury Police.

"If they can take five days not sleeping," he said, "we can take it"...

Conclusions

The government of El Salvador is making no real progress toward human rights.

The U.S. Embassy cites several developments as evidence that the government of El Salvador is moving forward. Officials point particularly to the amnesty and the formation of an official Human Rights Commission. As we have noted in our findings, both these actions have much more to do with public relations than human rights.

None of the current government parties offers a solution to El Salvador's ongoing conflict.

None of the trade unionists we spoke to in El Salvador had high hopes. The political parties that make up the current government have governed so incoherently that even centrist union leaders despair of any meaningful reform coming from these parties in the future.

We agree. The same factors that frustrate meaningful reform in El Salvador today will continue to frustrate reform.

Continued U.S. aid will not alter current political and military realities in El Salvador.

U.S. military officers readily admit that the FMLN forces who have taken up arms will not and cannot be defeated militarily by the Salvadoran government. There is, as we were told repeatedly by U.S. officials in San Salvador, no military solution.

If that is the case, we asked, why must the United States pursue a military course? The answer: "Because we have to convince the other side that *their* military strategy won't succeed."

In other words, we bankroll and outfit El Salvador's military machine in order to convince the other side victory can't be won. And if the other side remains unconvinced, what then? Still

He Killed Them All

I told him that many villagers had told me before that when the soldiers come into a village and arrest people, especially women, and then shoot them, what they didn't realize was that the little children who were watching them would never forget it. They would watch these soldiers shooting their mothers, and when they grew up, they would be thinking only of one thing: to get revenge on those soldiers. So they would join the guerrillas, not because they agreed with their politics, but because they wanted revenge. So maybe the best thing would be not to shoot these women . . .

Well, I had told him all that, and he hadn't interrupted me so I thought maybe my idea had worked. Then he nodded and he said only that maybe I was right about the little ones. And then the bastard made all the children go to their mothers, and gave the order to shoot. He killed them all. Seven women, four children, and one old man died in front of my eyes that afternoon. And God help me, it was my fault that those little babies were killed. If I had not said anything, not tried to be everybody's friend, those little ones would still be alive and playing under the sun.

Interview of Salvadoran, *The Progressive*, March, 1983, p. 41.

more military aid? An escalation of U.S. involvement? The current rationale behind our military policy in El Salvador cannot but lead us into another Vietnam.

Recommendations

Until there is an end to terror and respect for human rights, peace and democracy will be unattainable goals for El Salvador.

Given the history and record of U.S. intervention in El Salvador, we believe that a nonmilitary international presence is essential to prevent a regional escalation of adventurism and bloodshed.

We believe that such a nonmilitary international presence is a necessary precondition for the creation of a climate in which death squads cannot operate with impunity, free trade unions can be established and function, and the killers of religious and trade union activists can be brought to justice—by a judicial system that operates with a decent respect for the rights of all Salvadorans, rich and poor alike.

Specifically, we recommend that:

• the government of the United States support efforts by concerned Latin American and European nations to:

• restore a climate of respect for human rights inside El Salvador. Without such a climate, free elections are not possible . . .

• provide economic and humanitarian aid, under international auspices, that would serve the needs of the suffering people of El Salvador whatever their political preferences. The economic aid sent directly to the Salvadoran government so far has not reached those most in need.

• foster a dialogue—without prior conditions—among all representative political and economic factions in El Salvador, including the FDR-FMLN, to end the current violence and build a stable and democratic framework for political, social, and economic reconstruction . . .

During our entire stay in El Salvador, the most eloquent person we met may have been an official of the UCS (Unión Communal Salvadoreña), El Salvador's centrist peasant union. His words have stayed with us:

"To workers, to us at the bottom, the majority, all we have is the daily pain. We don't have a gun in our hand, and we don't have power to influence decisions. There should be peace, and, for that to happen, there must be dialogue. There must be dialogue between those who have guns."

Without that dialogue, there can be no peace in El Salvador.

GENOCIDE IN GUATEMALA

John Hammond

John Hammond, O.S.B., is prior of the benedictine monks of the Weston Priory in Weston, Vermont. This article relates the simple testimony from Guatemalan refugees in a Mexican village. It deals with the torture and murder of peasants by the Guatemalan military dictatorship.

Points To Consider

1. How had the Guatemalan refugees lived before fleeing to Mexico?
2. How did they describe the terror, torture and murder?
3. How were Guatemalan soldiers trained?
4. Why is the term "genocide" applied to events in Guatemala?

Reprinted with permission from **Sojourners**, P.O. Box 29272, Washington, D.C. 20017, December, 1983.

If the women would not tell, they were beaten and raped; children were abused and even dismembered within sight of their mothers.

During the month of February in 1983, five brothers of Weston Priory in Vermont took a journey to Mexico. We spent the month visiting Christian base communities with the Benedictine Missionary Sisters of Mexico. A visit with a small family community of Guatemalan refugees was for me the most moving event in our journey to Mexico . . .

They described how they had all lived as simple peasant farmers in a small Guatemalan village. Their life was poor, and they barely had enough to feed their children. Education and health care were luxuries granted only to the rich.

Stories began to reach their village about the Guatemalan military and its intrusions into nearby towns. The stories became increasingly terrifying. They were told that in one village the military commanded the people to kill the five leading catechists or else the whole village would be annihilated. All the people met to talk together. The five Christian leaders offered their lives rather than sacrificing the whole community. All formed in procession and went to the cemetery where the people shot their own leaders.

Word reached their village that the military were entering other towns, rounding up the women and children and asking the whereabouts of the men. If the women would not tell, they were beaten and raped; children were abused and even dismembered within sight of their mothers. The young men, often just teen-agers, were rounded up and conscripted into the army.

The terror became so intense and widespread that, at the news of the approach of the military, villagers of other communities fled in great numbers to the mountains. As they were fleeing, bombs were dropped on them from helicopters. The military would take over their villages, eat their food, kill their livestock, and burn their fields. Then they would wait while the people starved in the mountains, many of their children often freezing to death in the cold of night. The women told of the anguish of mothers whose infant children were smothered to death in their arms as they tried to stifle their crying so as not to be discovered by the soldiers.

As all these stories reached the village of this Guatemalan family, they became more and more terrified. Finally, the military arrived at their village. Two men were taken out of the vil-

25

lage by the soldiers. The next day the bodies of these men were found beside the road not far from the village.

A few days later a group of military visited again. This time they took five men. They stripped them and marched them off to a neighboring village where they were killed in front of all the people.

Realizing that they were to be next, the family gathered to see what they should do. Two of the husbands had already fled into the mountains in fear that they would be conscripted into the army on the next visit. The one remaining husband determined to take his wife and children with his two sisters-in-law and their children across the border into Mexico. The father of his wife chose to remain in the village to help those who could not leave.

The frightened family fled with whatever they could carry. They managed to cross the border and found a refugee camp in Mexico. But Guatemalan death squads were constantly crossing the border, seeking families whose men were suspected of being with the guerrillas or of supporting them. The family was moved to a town farther away where they would not be known or recognized.

Training soldiers

We asked the family how the soldiers, often taken from among the peasants themselves, could treat their own people so viciously.

The husband replied that one of his uncles had been in the military but had managed to leave it. He described the training of the young peasants. When a young man was inducted, he was first subjected to several days of starvation. Then a group of starving recruits would be gathered in a circle. A few tortillas would be placed in the center in front of them. They were then made to fight and brutalize one another to see who would get the tortilla to eat.

Similar "training" would then be given with live animals for bait. They would be taught to dismember the animals and eat them raw. At night they would be subjected to the blaring of loud-speakers telling them that the peasants were communists and the enemies of the country. After months of this kind of treatment, soldiers would become like brutes, with no sense of their humanity, and willing to perform any atrocities against their own people.

We asked why this was being done; for what purpose could the government of a people condone, let alone encourage, such action? Part of the answer came from the family, part from the priest who was aware of more of the political reality.

The family said that the government wanted to be rid of the guerrillas and were unable to do so directly because the guerrillas were able to hide in the hills. Often men would flee to the hills in order to escape the inhumanity of being inducted into the military. They could only survive, however, if the peasants fed and supported them.

The priest pointed out that 300 families control the wealth and

27

"Preserving Democracy"

Next year, 1984, will mark the 30th anniversary of military rule in Guatemala. In 1954 the Guatemalan army and its business allies took control of the country's government in a coup funded and directed by the United States Central Intelligence Agency. Since then the military has "preserved democracy" and Western ideals by killing tens of thousands of civilians, driving as many more into Mexican refugee camps, crushing the rural development movement, destroying the labor unions, controlling elections, and, more recently, nullifying the national constitution and disbanding the national congress. All the while it has enjoyed the fruits of widespread corruption . . .

In 1979 the Inter-American Development bank found that 59 per cent of Guatemala's national earnings went to the top five per cent of the population. In much of the rural area, 60 per cent of all children die before the age of five. An additional 25 per cent die before reaching the age of 15. According to the *Wall Street Journal*, only 50 per cent of Guatemalan Indian children have access to an elementary school education, and only one per cent of those ever go to high school.

Danna Martin, "A Change of Masks," *Sojourners*, November, 1983, p. 25.

resources of Guatemala. Two per cent of the population owns 80 per cent of the land. More than 60 per cent of the people are indigenous peasants who hold extremely small plots or no land at all. This Indian population has been exploited to the point of slavery, their families suffering from malnutrition and the deprivation of basic necessities at the hands of the large landowners.

The church, especially the priests and women religious, have helped the people to be aware of their human rights and dignity as people. Because of this, priests and religious, as well as at least two bishops, have been either killed or driven out of their parishes and dioceses. They have been replaced by fundamentalist ministers backed by U.S. funds and protected by the government.

These ministers preach a gospel of submission and acceptance of the present situation as the will of God for these poor people. They tell them that they must hope for a change only in the next life. They try to destroy any sense of solidarity and hope that has been built up by the church through the catechist leaders. Methodically, Christian leadership and influence on the social life of the people is being destroyed.

Genocide in Latin America

As this sad story was being recounted to us, my thoughts went back to the Jewish holocaust in Nazi Germany. I recalled that after the war I was discussing with a German monk the place of Christians and the church in the extermination of Jews in Germany. The monk said, "Well, we didn't really realize what was going on right under our noses. We believed our government when they told us that what they were doing was for the good of our country."

I could not help but think of the parallel. Genocide is going on in Latin America. Directly or indirectly, our own government is supplying advisers, bombs, planes, spare parts—all being used to exterminate a people. The weapons are made by our hands, paid for with our money. Our government is telling us that what it is doing is for the good of our country.

A few years from now, if the earth is still "civilized" and inhabitable, will a monk from Germany be asking a North American monk, "How could that happen? What were Christians doing, thinking? Where were you? Where was the church?"

The young mother concluded our visit telling us of the death of her father. She had received the news two weeks previously when one of her relatives, who had walked the long, perilous way from Guatemala, visited.

Her father had been visiting with two young men in his dwelling in the village. A group of military arrived outside. One young man volunteered to go to see what they wanted. As he stepped outside, they shot him. The other young man fled out through the roof while the woman's father held the military off with a pistol. The young man escaped to the hills; the father was shot to death.

As the woman concluded her story, the Mexican priest turned to her and said, "But you see, all North American people are not your enemies, and they are not all evil. They do not want your people to suffer and die; it is their government which encourages this evil. Look at these brothers. They are North Americans, and they are your brothers. There are many more like them. Tell them what you want from them."

The woman with the infant in her arms told us with tears, but without bitterness or despair, "We know that all your people are not evil. Please tell them to stop their government from sending arms; they only kill our people."

The story I have told is the simple story of defenseless people who had no reason to distort the truth. We promised to tell the story. I pray that their voice will be heard.

A NATION OF PRISONERS

Orville Schell

Orville Schell is the chairman of Americas Watch. The Watch Committees watch human rights practices. The Helsinki Watch focuses on human rights in the 35 countries in Eastern and Western Europe and North America that signed the 1975 Helsinki accords on security and cooperation in Europe. The Americas Watch is concerned with human rights in the nations of Central and South America and the Caribbean.

In addition, both Committees watch the foreign policy of the United States to determine whether it reflects the U.S. commitment to human rights and helps promote respect for human rights in other countries. They are concerned with fundamental rights that are guaranteed in several international agreements—among them, the 1969 American Convention on Human Rights, and the 1975 Helsinki Final Act.

Points To Consider

1. How was the oppression of Indian people described?
2. How many Guatemalan Indians have fled to Mexico?
3. What is said about U.S. military aid to Guatemala?
4. How is a human rights solution for Central America defined?

Excerpted from testimony presented by Americas Watch before the National Bipartisan Commission on Central America, 1984. Henry Kissinger was the chairman of this committee.

The world holds us directly responsible for their murders, their disappearances, their torture. Unless we commit ourselves to a human rights solution, it is a responsibility we cannot evade.

In Guatemala, though the practices of the armed forces have not been so exhaustively documented as in El Salvador because of the absence of any domestic human rights group operating within the country, the available evidence indicates that overwhelming human rights abuses continue. Up to a few months ago, rural massacres were taking place in which entire Indian villages were destroyed and their populations were wiped out. Disappearances in Guatemala City, which subsided during the early months of the Rios Montt regime, have resumed in quantity. Again, the government's policy is terror. Even in sections of the country that appear to have been "pacified," it is a "peace" that has been imposed and that is maintained by terror. To the best of our knowledge, no effort is underway to punish those responsible for massacring Indians. 100,000 Guatemalan Indians have fled to Southern Mexico and many hundreds of thousands are displaced persons in their own country.

Though the United States is far less centrally involved in Guatemala than in El Salvador, our support provides the only veneer of legitimacy to what should be a pariah nation. We make it possible for governments that depend on us, such as those of Taiwan and Israel, to supply its military needs. We should end all military aid to Guatemala, and all economic aid except for aid to meet basic human needs, and we should organize an international arms boycott. It should end only when there is clear and convincing evidence that the Guatemalan armed forces are not practicing terror against the Guatemalan Indians.

National security

Having stated our view that we believe that our national security would be enhanced by our identification with the cause of human rights for the people of Guatemala and El Salvador, let me now turn to those who object that the human rights situation would not improve if we withdrew our sponsorship of those governments.

● It is objected that, though those governments are terrible, the Marxist-Leninist governments that would take their place if the guerrillas prevail could be even worse.

32

I resent these unfounded accusations!

In answering that objection, it must first be pointed out that it is hard to conceive anything worse than the governments of El Salvador and Guatemala. Matters may well be so far gone in El Salvador that, without our support, a Marxist revolution will prevail. That seems far less likely in Guatemala, but it is also a possibility. If that happens, it would certainly be undesirable. The human rights situation will be bad, but hardly worse . . .

As for the government of Guatemala, we can only guess at how many Indians it has killed. Perhaps something worse is possible, but that possibility does not seem a compelling reason for

33

Before My Very Eyes

What torture did you see them inflict on the others?

Several. Electric shocks between the water troughs. They put a hood on one of them with quicklime in it. They pulled one up by his testicles; I also saw them pull a boy of about 17 by his testicles and an officer slashed his jaw in two with his knife; and he cut his wrists to the bone; but I suppose although the boy screamed at first he stopped later because he'd fainted. I also saw another boy they had handcuffed with his hands behind his back; they also locked his feet together then lifted him up between the two of them and dropped him. I saw his teeth drop out and gushes of blood—that's how they break your ribs—from the way you fall—and that's when they give you the worst kicks. That's what they did to me—that is, they didn't lift me up but they kicked me in the ribs, the mouth, the stomach until I passed out.

How did they torture you?

They pulled me up by my testicles; and they hooded me with quicklime—that means they put a bit of quicklime inside the inner tube of a truck tyre, then they put it over your nose and then they roll it onto you and you feel like death itself until you pass out, or, well, you tell some lies or the truth if you don't know. [sic]

Did they kill anyone in your presence? If so, how?

Yes, before my very eyes they killed three people; they strangled them. The way they killed them was with a piece of rope, a kind of noose, which they put round the neck and then used a stick to tighten it like a tourniquet from behind—handcuffed, and with their heads held down in the trough. When they came, their eyes were open; they'd already turned purple. It took at most three minutes in the water. I also saw that

34

Continued on next page

> one of these three, a boy, when they threw him down on the floor with his clothes wet, was still moving and one of the officers ordered them to put the tourniquet on him again until he stopped moving.
>
> They just showed me the other six bodies and said the same thing would happen to me if I tried to lie to them.
>
> Amnesty International, Guatemala: *A Government Program of Political Murder*, 1981.

us to support and identify ourselves with such murderous governments . . .

We are not asserting, of course, that identification with human rights is the only component of national security. We are asserting, however, that identification with human rights is an essential element of our national security . . .

Increasingly, prominent voices are heard calling for a military solution to the problems of Central America. In the view of Americas Watch, such a solution would only compound the disaster of the region.

Reject military solution

We call on you to reject a military solution and to endorse a human rights solution, both because it is right and because we believe that it would serve the interests of the United States. Nothing else would bring so much credit to the United States in Central America, in the rest of Latin America, in the world, and with the American people. We recognize that the United States is allied with repressive regimes in many parts of the world—in Pakistan, in Turkey, in South Korea, and in the Philippines—and that those alliances dilute our claim to stand for human rights against Soviet totalitarianism. But the damage is far greater to us from our support for repressive regimes in central America because our identification with those regimes is far greater. The world holds us directly responsible for their murders, their disappearances, their torture. American citizens also hold us responsible for their murders, their disappearances, their torture. Unless we commit ourselves to a human rights solution, it is a responsibility we cannot evade.

35

They Killed The Boy

Did they kill that boy too?
Yes, what they said to him was, if you don't talk, we'll kill you.

But was he killed?
No, I didn't kill him.

No, but did the others kill this boy?
Oh yes, definitely; he confessed: "I confess everything, everything"—that he wasn't a guerrilla or anything, but, in any case, they began to beat him, that is to torture him, and they even tried to knock out one of his teeth like this, with a hammer. They hit him with a hammer like this. He screamed. They even smashed his finger. They put it on a piece of iron and hit it with the hammer to make him talk; but he didn't say anything: Then at midnight they took those men who were there; they just went and grabbed them by the hair and feet and threw them into a car and took them away—took them who knows where. (From an interview with a former government soldier.)

Amnesty International, *Guatemala: A Government Program of Political Murder,* 1981.

RECOGNIZING AUTHOR'S POINT OF VIEW

This activity may be used as an individualized study guide for students in libraries and resource centers or as a discussion catalyst in small group and classroom discussions.

Many readers are unaware that written material usually expresses an opinion or bias. The capacity to recognize an author's point of view is an essential reading skill. The skill to read with insight and understanding involves the ability to detect different kinds of opinions or bias. Sex bias, race bias, ethnocentric bias, political bias and religious bias are five basic kinds of opinions expressed in editorials and all literature that attempts to persuade. They are briefly defined in the glossary below.

FIVE KINDS OF EDITORIAL OPINION OR BIAS

*sex bias—the expression of dislike for and/or feeling of superiority over the opposite sex or a particular sexual minority

*race bias—the expression of dislike for and/or feeling of superiority over a racial group

*ethnocentric bias—the expression of a belief that one's own group, race, religion, culture or nation is superior. Ethnocentric persons judge others by their own standards and values

*political bias—the expression of political opinions and attitudes about domestic or foreign affairs

*religious bias—the expression of a religious belief or attitude

Guidelines

1. Locate three examples of political opinion or bias in the readings from chapter one.

2. Locate five sentences that provide examples of **any kind** of editorial opinion or bias from the readings in chapter one.

37

3. Write down each of the sentences referred to in guideline two and determine what kind of bias each sentence represents. Is it **sex bias, race bias, ethnocentric bias, political bias,** or **religious bias?**

4. Make up one sentence statements that would be an example of each of the following: **sex bias, race bias, ethnocentric bias, political bias** and **religious bias.**

5. See if you can locate five sentences that are factual statements from the readings in chapter one.

6. Summarize the author's point of view in one sentence for each of the readings in chapter one of this book:

Reading 1 _____

_____

Reading 2 _____

_____

Reading 3 _____

_____

Reading 4 _____

_____

CHAPTER 2

TERROR ON THE LEFT: COMMUNIST VIOLENCE IN CENTRAL AMERICA

5 READING

SANDINISTA HUMAN RIGHTS VIOLATIONS

U.S. State Department Report

The following statement was excerpted from the Country Reports on Human Rights *publication done by the U.S. State Department. This report was submitted to the Senate and House Committees on Foreign Relations. This article was excerpted from the section on El Salvador. Reports were made on all nations.*

Points To Consider

1. How is the FSLN described?
2. What happened to the Miskito Indians?
3. What is said about killing, disappearance and torture?
4. What is the status of the free press and speech?

Excerpted from the U.S. State Department's **Country Reports on Human Rights** issued in February, 1983.

Miskito leaders have documented incidents of forced marches, tortures, and executions of Indians by government forces.

The National Directorate of the Sandinista National Liberation Front (FSLN), a group of nine Marxist revolutionary leaders who took control in July 1979, holds political power in Nicaragua. A three-man junta, consisting of one of the FSLN National Directorate commanders and two civilians, serves as head of government. Although it maintains that it is committed to pluralism and a mixed economy, the FSLN has progressively consolidated its power and restricted civil liberties.

The human rights situation deteriorated markedly in 1982. Freedom House listed Nicaragua in its study among those countries where there was a significant decline in freedom. Early in the year, the Government of National Reconstruction forcibly moved thousands of Miskito Indians from their traditional homes along the river boundary with Honduras to camps in the interior, claiming that it had done so in reaction to an outbreak of anti-government armed violence. Between 11,000 and 14,000 Indians fled to Honduras. Many villages were burned and animals belonging to the Indians slaughtered. Miskito leaders have documented incidents of forced marches, tortures, and executions of Indians by government forces. The Miskitos have not been permitted to return to their traditional homes. The Nicaraguan Roman Catholic Bishops' Conference in February 1982 publicly condemned the methods employed to move the Miskitos.

In March, the Government declared a state of emergency, claiming an imminent threat of invasion after anti-Sandinistas blew up two bridges. In fact the Government is facing several areas of significant guerrilla activity. The state of emergency suspended many civil liberties guaranteed in the Statute on Rights and Guarantees, the basic law guaranteeing personal and civil liberties decreed by the revolutionary Government in August 1979 . . .

Killing

There is credible evidence that security forces have been responsible for the death of a number of detained persons . . .

There have also been reports of kidnappings and executions of Miskito Indians by anti-Sandinista forces. The Government claimed that in 1982 anti-Sandinistas killed at least 253 members of security forces and civilians and claimed to have killed 375 of

41

its armed opponents and captured 76. Most of these casualties reportedly occurred in clashes between opposing armed groups.

In November and December of 1982, there were credible reports of security officials killing at least 10 prisoners. In some cases, individuals were arrested by the Government and not heard from until their names appeared in lists of dead "counter-revolutionaries." In another case, a prisoner died of gunshot wounds the day before he was to be released. The Government announced that the prisoner had committed suicide.

Disappearance

In the first nine months of 1982, the independent Permanent Human Rights Commission documented 20 cases of disappearances under circumstances which indicated security forces were involved. In 15 cases the individuals have been located. Five cases are still unresolved.

Torture

Torture is not widely practiced by the Government. There have been, however, at least half a dozen documented cases of torture committed by security forces in 1982. In the most notorious case, a taxi driver, who the Interior Ministry claimed was killed while attempting to escape, was tortured and then shot at close range. In one case the Government investigated and punished police officials who abused prisoners in the town of Granada. The prisoners, charged with common crimes, were later set

42

free by the courts because of the abuse they had suffered under detention. In the case of the tortured-murdered taxi driver, the Supreme Court has requested a full investigation from the Government. State security regularly uses sophisticated methods of psychological interrogation. There are credible reports of prisoners under interrogation being forced to remain nude, threatened with the death of members of their family, and subjected to other types of psychological abuse. In some instances, the prisoners have been beaten.

Cruel, inhuman, or degrading treatment or punishment

The Government currently holds about 7,000 prisoners. About 3,600 of these can be considered political prisoners, most of whom are ex-members of the National Guard who were convicted by special tribunals. Overcrowding and substandard conditions remain serious problems which the Government acknowledges and attributes to its limited resources . . .

Some prisoner abuse has continued. After several prisoners escaped from a penitentiary, their colleagues remaining in that prison were forced to work nude and their families were denied visitation rights for several months.

Revolutionary Terror

Rep. Siljander noted that "the revolutionary, terrorist left keeps right on killing soldiers and civilians, bombing bridges and power lines, leaving innocent people dead, in the dark, or out of work." He said the guerrillas realize they can obtain power only "through the barrel of a gun, or through deception, or through a combination of both."

Rep. Solomon challenged the media to examine the evidence. "As it is now," he said, "these violations are not being fully explored by the Western media, which have been blinded by their obsession with human rights violations by government security forces and so-called right-wing death squads."

Human Events Editorial, 1983

Arbitrary arrest and imprisonment

Nicaraguan law guarantees that a prisoner will not be held by police for more than seven days or state security more than 48 hours before his case is presented to a judge. These rights, however, were suspended by the state of emergency in March 1982. Consequently, arbitrary detention has dramatically increased. State security has detained without due process hundreds of suspected anti-Sandinistas. Some have been released after a few days, others after a few weeks. Scores are still being held.

The right of habeas corpus, guaranteed in the statute of rights and guarantees, has been suspended by the state of emergency.

Denial of fair public trial

In theory, the judicial system operates independently in Nicaragua and there are few complaints that those accused of common crimes have not received a fair trial. However, in the case of those charged with violating the law of maintenance of public order and security, the judges usually base the sentence on the findings of the Government interrogators. Military personnel or civilians accused of participating in a crime involving a member of the military are tried by military rather than civilian courts. Civilians tried by military courts are not subject to the guarantees of the civilian judicial system, though they are allowed to be represented by counsel, but may appeal to the Supreme Court. Although there is provision for legal counsel for military defendants, in practice, many do not receive adequate legal assistance. Sentences imposed by the military courts, generally for crimes of desertion, robbery, and assault are severe, varying in those cases between 18 and 26 years. It is estimated that 40 to 50 civilians are in military jails . . .

Freedom of speech and press

Both the printed and spoken media are now subject to prior censorship. The censors are arbitrary and capricious, removing virtually all references to activities of the external opposition, as well as many articles implicitly critical of government policies or programs.

All independent newscasts were prohibited for the first three months of the state of emergency and a single government-run radio news program was broadcast by all stations. In June, several pro-government radio stations and one independent radio station were permitted to broadcast their own news programs, but the remaining radio stations are still prohibited from broadcasting independent news or political programs. The Government controls the only two television stations and non-Sandinista groups are denied access to television.

One of the three daily newspapers is the official voice of the FSLN; another is pro-government. There have been several cases this year of journalists being harassed, beaten and intimidated . . .

Since the imposition of the state of emergency, it has been very difficult for the opposition to make any of its views known publicly, although occasionally the censors have permitted some articles reflecting opposition viewpoints. The Government permits in its own papers some criticism of lower ranking bureaucrats, but no criticism of the FSLN leadership and their policies is allowed.

While there is no censorship of domestic or imported books, the foreign exchange crisis has meant that few books from the West are imported into Nicaragua, while Marxist literature circulates freely. The "curriculum rationalization and coordination" imposed on the National Autonomous University and the Catholic University of Central America is a government measure which has limited the universities' autonomy in developing the curriculum and has circumscribed university freedom. Moreover, the choice of textbooks is limited, as described above, and, in the social sciences, texts with a high ideological content are used. Nevertheless, the universities retain a significant degree of independence in naming their faculties.

COMRADES KILL EACH OTHER

Fred Schwarz

Fred Schwarz is the author and publisher of the Christian Anti-Communism Crusade. *His weekly newsletter warns of the dangers of communism. Fred Schwarz is a former physician who for some years has devoted full time to his newsletter. His publication warns about what is termed the "world-wide threat of communism."*

Points To Consider

1. Who was Anaya Montes and how was she killed?
2. What was the motive for her murder?
3. How is the communist attitude toward killing described?
4. How are communist leaders described?

Fred Schwarz, "Communist Cannibalism," **Christian Anti-Communist Crusade**, August 1, 1983.

The communist attitude towards killing is remarkably casual. Communist literature abounds with the advocacy of death for those considered enemies or rivals.

How these comrades kill one another!

"The murderers dressed themselves in hoods and wore rubber gloves to commit the crime, according to Nicaraguan police. For weapons they used knives and ice picks, stabbing Anaya Montes more than 80 times and then cutting her throat." (Guardian, May 4, page 12)

Despite the similarities, this is not a killing by a group aping the Manson gang, nor by an escaped convict who was previously an escapee from a mental hospital. This is a political assassination of a comrade by comrades. It describes the murder of Dr. Anaya Montes, known as Commander Ana Maria, who was the second-in-command of the Popular Liberation Forces (FPL) in El Salvador by Rogelio A. Bazzaglia Recinos, a member of the FPL Central Command.

This murder, which took place on April 6 in Managua, has caused both consternation and debate among the supporters of the Revolutionary forces in El Salvador. The FPL is the largest and most militant guerrilla organization in that country. It was formed and led by the legendary Commander Marcial, whose real name was Salvador Cayetano Carpio. When the commander-in-chief learned that his second-in-command had been murdered by one of his commanders, he committed suicide . . .

The motive for the murder was a policy difference between the murderer and the victim.

Casual killing

The communist attitude towards killing is remarkably casual. Communist literature abounds with the advocacy of death for those considered enemies or rivals. Marching delegations of communists carry banners with such slogans as: "Death to the Klan"; "Death to the Imperialists". Communist reporters exalt when their opponents suffer physical injury, and after riotous conflict, proudly brag that: "We sent ten of them to hospital", or lament their inability to attain their objectives with such statements as, "The police stopped us killing them."

This casual attitude to killing has a long tradition in communist circles. It is sanctified by Lenin's own attitude. His attitude to killing is clearly revealed in an article he wrote and distributed in 1918 and which is still published proudly by the Soviet authori-

Peasants in El Salvador

ties. It is entitled, "How to Organize Competition," and he presents haphazard killing as one way of providing an incentive to make others work. He states:

"Thousands of practical forms and methods of accounting and controlling the rich, the rogues and the idlers should be devised and put to a practical test by the communes themselves, by small units in town and country. Variety is a guarantee of virility here, a pledge of success in achieving the single common aim—to purge the land of Russia of all vermin, of fleas—the rogues, of bugs—the rich, and so on and so forth. In one place half a score of rich, a dozen rogues, half a dozen workers who shirk their work (in the hooligan manner in which many compositors in Petrograd, particularly in the Party printing shops, shirk their work) will be put in prison. In another place they will be put to cleaning latrines. In a third place they will be provided
48

with 'yellow tickets' after they have served their time, so that all the people shall have them under surveillance, as harmful persons, until they reform. In a fourth place, one out of every ten idlers will be shot on the spot. *In a fifth place mixed methods may be adopted, and by probational release, for example, the rich, the bourgeois intellectuals, the rogues and hooligans who are corrigible will be given an opportunity to reform quickly. The more variety there will be, the better and richer will be our general experience, the more certain and rapid will be the success of Socialism."* (V. I. Lenin, Selected Works. Foreign Languages Publishing House, Moscow, pages 376–377)

In the U.S.A. the communist tradition of advocating mass killing is maintained and proclaimed by the Progressive Labor Party and the Revolutionary Communist Party. The Communist Party (USA) and the Socialist Workers Party are relatively silent on the issue. Nevertheless, they are inheritors of the same tradition and believers in the same doctrines which justify and even demand class extermination.

The root—atheism

The roots of this communist attitude to killing are their doctrines of atheism and materialism. Marxist doctrine affirms that there is no God and that every human being is temporary and totally material. Since a human body is one of countless millions that have been created by evolution throughout the aeons of history, an individual is like the white foam on the crest of a curling wave—destined to sparkle in the sunlight for a moment and then disappear forever. To hesitate to hasten the inevitable end of such temporary fortuitous creatures, when the greatest of causes demands it, would be treason to history.

Equally Repugnant

One axiom must not be lost: The death squads and the leftists are not equally objectionable (they are equally repugnant), for the simple reason that the agenda of the right-wing thugs stops at the border. They do not take orders from Cuba and Russia; they do not have designs on Honduras, Guatemala, Mexico. However ghastly their behavior, they do not threaten our strategic interests.

National Review Editorial, 1984

There are many "Pol Pots" lurking in the communist bushes who believe this and are ready to apply it should they have the opportunity.

Atheism bears bitter fruit. As the Psalmist says: *"The fool has said in his heart, there is no God. They are corrupt. They have done abominable works. There is none that doest good."*

Cannibalism

Revolutions have a habit of devouring their own children, and this is particularly true of communist revolutions. Communist leaders are passionate ideologues and potential megalomaniacs. They believe that the communist party is the chosen instrument of history and that it has been given the sublime responsibility of leading the masses of mankind into the promised land of proletarian dictatorship. The simple fact that this individual has risen to a position of power in such a party proves that he is one of history's elect. When the competitor advocates a policy that will delay communist victory—shoot him down. It matters not that he has been a friend and colleague for many years.

Obeying this mandate of history, Stalin exterminated the majority of the Bolsheviks who conquered Russia; Mao Zedong tortured and humiliated the majority of the communists who conquered China (via the Great Cultural Revolution), and Commander Recinos murdered Commander Anaya Montes, second-in-command of the Popular Liberation Forces of El Salvador.

The future of the U.S.A.

Fanatical ideologues can and do commit the most monstrous crimes with a clear conscience.

It is unlikely that Hitler's conscience troubled him as he conceived and directed the holocaust; there is no evidence that Stalin was consumed with debilitating doubt as he ordered the torture and death of his old comrades; and Pol Pot was convinced that he was doing his historic duty as the tragic procession of the tormented and dying moved out of Phnom Penh.

Should the communists conquer the U.S.A., their leaders will also have a duty to perform. Mankind must be regenerated. The diseased human cattle must be eliminated, the bourgeoisie must be liquidated. Fanatical communists have killed millions in the past, and they will doubtless do so in the future. Those who will not learn the lessons of history are condemned to repeat them.

I look upon the beautiful faces and laughing eyes of my grandchildren, and my heart sings. I think of the deadly communist doctrines, the history of communist murder, and the increasingly successful communist program for the conquest of the U.S.A., and I tremble. No sacrifice is too great to prevent communist victory.

50

7

TERROR ON THE LEFT

GUERILLA TERROR IN EL SALVADOR

Norman C. Mintle

Norman C. Mintle was reared by missionary parents in Honduras, Central America. He earned his Bachelor of Arts degree in communications and Spanish from Evangel College, Springfield, Missouri, and took a Master of Arts degree in communications from Western Michigan University, Kalamazoo, in 1975. His understanding of Latin American culture paved the way for him to become ranking specialist for Latin American affairs for Dr. Pat Robertson and the Christian Broadcasting Network. Mintle has recently traveled to Latin America on three occasions, visiting eight countries and coordinating more than a thousand man-hours of investigative research.

Points To Consider

1. Who did the author speak with in the refugee camp?
2. Why is the war strategy defined as humane?
3. What is said about right wing and left wing death squads?
4. Why has the "true story" about El Salvador not been getting to the American people?

Excerpted from the testimony by Norman C. Mintle before the Joint Hearing of the Western Hemisphere Affairs and Human Rights Subcommittees, February 21, 1984.

51

The guerillas on the left are, by their very nature and purpose, death squads.

In the refugee camp in San Vicente, I spoke with a young mother who had been routed from her home, three years earlier, fearing for her life and the lives of her children. She was not politically aware enough to have an opinion about the elections. All she wanted, she told me, was to go back to her home in the valley, without fear of guerilla attacks, and raise fruit in her yard once again.

In that same refugee camp I asked a teenage boy why he had to leave home. He seemed uneasy about answering me directly, and would only say, "The man made me go." When I pressed him as to the man's identity, he finally responded, "Guerillas."

In the cities, the police attempt to maintain urban peace by routinely stopping incoming buses and other vehicles at random, searching for terrorists and their weapons. We observed that the people, far from being angered by the interruptions, actually appreciate the efforts of the police, in spite of the inconvenience—because the people are committed to peace.

There is good and healthy progress in El Salvador. The much maligned land reform program, initiated by the revolutionary junta of 1979, is moving forward steadily. It is a massive job, something akin to taking the two hundred largest ranches in the American West away from their owners and distributing them among thousands and thousands of farmhands. In El Salvador this is a worthy project, but patience needs to be our watchword . . .

The war

This war could have been fought in one of several ways. A lieutenant colonel in the Salvadoran Army pointed out to me that the conflict could be over in a matter of days. Simply bombing known insurgent strongholds would eliminate the problem quickly. But by that method, thousands of innocent civilians would die, and the Army has consciously made the moral decision not to sacrifice human life unnecessarily. Instead, they have opted for an appropriate, humane strategy, which first defends the lives of the country's citizens, then protects the crucial life-support system of the people—the bridges, the farms, the hydroelectric plants, the sugar cane factories—and finally responds to crises precipitated by the terrorists.

Obviously, the death squads exist, and they are often comprised of members of the armed forces. A plainclothes military officer told me that death squads customarily recruit from

52

among the bitterest and most disgruntled members of a unit, those who have suffered the deepest personal losses through the war . . .

Guerillas routinely kill

A point, however, must be made. The world press routinely ascribes virtually every killing in El Salvador to the work of right-wing death squads, when in fact the guerillas on the left are, by their very nature and purpose, death squads. The guerillas routinely kill innocent people, as well as each other—and there is dissension in their ranks because of it.

We interviewed a young guerilla, captured just four days before, named Jose Guadalupe Hernandez Garcia. Without his captors present, he told us of brutality within the guerilla ranks. Foodstuffs are often in such short supply, he said, that guerillas raid the homes of innocent campesinos, some of whom are murdered if they resist in the slightest way. Thousands are driven out into the refugee camps. This young guerilla recounted one incident in which his own unit, virtually starving to death in the mountains, came to the home of an old woman living alone to beg or steal food. The impoverished old senora herself had nothing to eat, and the commanding officer of the unit, Ricardo Beltran, in his frustration ordered her to be shot on sight.

The Liberal Bias

Few things show the liberals' bias so much as their phony demand for "human rights" in El Salvador. That beleaguered nation did have an election . . . and voted anti-Communist even though they were under the terrorist threat of "vote in the morning and die at night."

The liberals crying about "human rights" in El Salvador are the same people who told us that Chiang Kai-shek was corrupt and reactionary while Mao-Tse-tung was an agrarian reformer; and now we have Communist China. The liberals told us that Batista was corrupt and reactionary while Castro was an agrarian reformer; and now we have Communist Cuba.

The *Phyllis Schlafly Report*, 1983

The guerillas' lack of respect for human life extends to their own troops. Hernandez Garcia told of his comrades killing wounded members of their own units if they were unable to keep up. He also explained how guerilla fighters are recruited: in his own unit of seven hundred, more than two hundred, he said, had been kidnapped and forced into servitude. Indeed, twenty-four others in Hernandez Garcia's unit had laid plans to defect from the guerilla movement on the very night after his capture.

Clearly, the left has lost its vital base of popular support . . .

The true story

The American people are not getting the true story. Few Americans, for example, have been told by our news media that you gentlemen of the Congress have approved three times more economic aid than military aid for El Salvador. Few Americans have been told by the news media that guerilla forces actually control only the slightest sliver of Salvadoran territory. Few Americans have been told by the news media that the armed forces of El Salvador are confident of winning, and are indeed winning, this conflict. In fact, for some reason, the only battle that the leftist guerillas are winning is the battle being waged in the American media.

Our press has reported a story. The American people ought to have the facts.

TERROR ON THE LEFT

IN SEARCH OF DEATH SQUADS

M. Stanton Evans

M. Stanton Evans is a nationally syndicated columnist, speaker and writer. He is a frequent contributor to **Human Events** *and other conservative newspapers and magazines of social and political opinion.*

Points To Consider

1. How is major media coverage of violence in El Salvador described?
2. What is the "truth of the matter?"
3. Why does the author say killings by the left are more numerous than killings by the right?
4. What is meant by right and left wing groups?

M. Stanton Evans, "In Search of Death Squads," **Human Events**, March 31, 1984, p. 7.

55

The Communist terrorists operating in El Salvador are among the most ruthless in the world.

The question for today is: Can there be such a thing as a left-wing "death squad"?

If we are to believe the coverage given by the major media to the bloody conflict in El Salvador, the answer is an obvious "no." Even though a terrorist war is raging there in which casualties are inflicted daily by both sides, the "death squad" epithet is applied exclusively to the anti-Communist government and the right, never to the Communists or others on the left.

The Washington Post

Consider the commentary on this topic in a recent (March 15) issue of the Washington *Post*. In a story about the El Salvador elections, the *Post* provides repeated references to "right-wing assassination teams," "death squads," "death squad killings," "right-wing violence," "the violent right," and "vigilante gangs"—all alluding to anti-Communist forces in the country.

The same article also contains several references to Salvadoran Communist forces, but the words "death squads," "violence," "killings," or "gangs" are never applied to them. The terms employed instead are "left-wing guerrillas," a "strong left-wing insurgency," "the guerrillas," and "the left." Not only are these forces never described as murderers, they also aren't described as Communists (though they make no particular secret of this fact).

Thus the words applied to the anti-Communists are uniformly negative, calculated to arouse distaste and fear. The words applied to the Communists range from blandly neutral to legitimizing: The right consists of "death squads" while the left is just a "strong insurgency." This pattern holds even in stories specifically concerned with left-wing assassinations in which the anti-Communists are victims.

The very same issue of the *Post* quoted above contains a story about the murder of conservative Salvadoran deputy Hector Flores Larin, the third conservative member of the legislature murdered in recent months.

At no point in this story does the *Post* refer to the killers of Flores Larin or the other conservative deputies as "death squads." Instead, it tells us U.S. officials have "blamed left-wing guerrillas for the earlier killings" and that "a left-wing guerrilla group, the Workers Revolutionary Movement, said it killed" Flo-
56

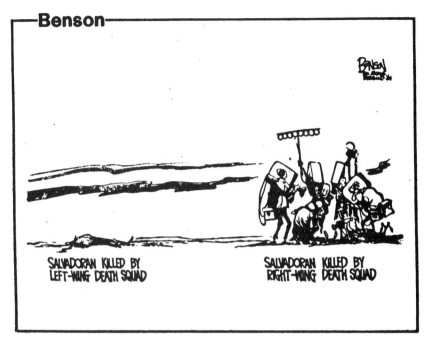

SALVADORAN KILLED BY
LEFT-WING DEATH SQUAD

SALVADORAN KILLED BY
RIGHT-WING DEATH SQUAD

res Larin. All of this in the self-same issue that talks at length about the "right-wing death squads" of El Salvador.

The next day the *Post* surpassed even this performance, reporting yet another assassination committed by the Salvadoran Communists. This was a particularly atrocious crime, since the killers not only murdered conservative political figure Tito Adelberto Rosa, but also shot and critically wounded his four-year-old daughter whom he was driving to school. The self-proclaimed killers, the *Post* blandly informs us, were "a guerrilla group" on the left. Again, the left-wing assassins are conspicuously not described as "death squads." In addition, the *Post* takes pains to suggest this cold-blooded murder was not attributable to the main body of Communist guerrillas (describing the murderers as a "breakaway" group).

The *Post* does not point out that such killings are fairly routine for the Communists, but does go out of its way to say "a number of deaths of leftist and centrist political figures have been attributed to the extreme right and government forces."

In short, every rhetorical stop is pulled to slant such stories in favor of the Communists and against the anti-Communists, even when the specific subject being covered is a murder committed by the left. The net effect is to suggest it is the right that is

57

chiefly responsible for violence in El Salvador, and that any such action by the left is merely an aberration.

Communist terror

The truth of the matter is precisely the opposite. The Communist terrorists operating in El Salvador are among the most ruthless in the world (they have been known to murder each other), and the counter-violence coming from the anti-Communist side is a result of the fear and chaos the terrorists create. This is, of course, a major object of left-wing terrorism, spelled out in all the manuals. (The idea is to provoke the target government to reprisals that will lend itself to de-legitimizing outcry over human rights.)

Moreover, killings by the left are more numerous than killings on the right. According to data cited in 1982 by the House Intelligence Committee of attributable political killings in El Salvador, 14 per cent were traceable to left-wing terrorists, 13 per cent to government security forces, and 2 per cent to right-wing terrorists. Reports from the Foreign Broadcast Information Service indicate 300 killings a month attributable to the left. The Salvador Human Rights Commission found, in the first six months of 1983, 10 times as many non-combatant killings by the left as by the anti-Communists.

You would never know any of this, however, from reading the Washington *Post*—which locates the Salvadoran "death squads" exclusively on the right.

"Death Squads"

"Death Squads" is a term reserved for those who kill in the cause of saving a centrist or right-wing regime. If you wish a general absolution for murder in this modern age, you must explain that you are killing "reactionaries" to advance the people's revolution.

The most successful tactic, for example, of the guerrillas in El Salvador is to use the element of surprise, shoot the peasant-soldiers guarding some installation or village, execute the local officials supporting the government, propagandize the peasants, and move on.

Patrick J. Buchanan, 1984

INTERPRETING
EDITORIAL CARTOONS

This activity may be used as an individualized study guide for students in libraries and resource centers or as a discussion catalyst in small group and classroom discussions.

Although cartoons are usually humorous, the main intent of most political cartoonists is not to entertain. Cartoons express serious social comment about important issues. Using graphic and visual arts, the cartoonist expresses opinions and attitudes. By employing an entertaining and often light-hearted visual format, cartoonists may have as much or more impact on national and world issues as editorial and syndicated columnists.

Points to consider

1. Examine the two cartoons in this activity.

2. How would you describe the message of each cartoon? Try to describe each message in one to three sentences.

Reprinted with permission of *The Minneapolis Star and Tribune.*

3. Do you agree with the message expressed in either cartoon? Why or why not?

4. Are any of the readings in chapter two in basic agreement with either of the cartoons? Why or why not?

5. Which reading in chapter one would be in basic agreement with the cartoon's message?

CHAPTER 3

THE DEATH SQUADS AND U.S. POLICY: POINTS AND COUNTERPOINTS

READINGS

9 READING

SUPPORTING THE DEATH SQUADS

Robert White

Robert White was the United States Ambassador to El Salvador during the Carter Administration. He was replaced as Ambassador to El Salvador by the Reagan Administration. He now works and writes for the Commission on United States-Central American Relations.

Points To Consider

1. Why do conditions justify recourse to revolution in Central America?
2. What has been the fundamental error of U.S. policy in El Salvador?
3. What is the nature of the ARENA party?
4. Who is Roberto D'Aubuisson?
5. What actions would bring about peace?

Excerpted from testimony by Robert White before the House Subcommittee on Western Hemisphere Affairs, February 2, 1984.

When leaders for human dignity and change—men such as Archbishop Oscar Romero and Land Reform Chief Roldolfo Viera—continued their efforts on behalf of the poor, military death squads gunned them down.

Only strong action can give hope that civilian murder in El Salvador will be reduced. To understand this, one must understand the inner-workings of violence in El Salvador . . .

The ragtag forces of revolution deal blow after staggering blow to an American trained and supplied military force . . . Given the miserable record of the forces we support, is it not past time to stop throwing guns and money at the problem and ask why?

Any formulation of a national policy toward Central America must begin with the recognition that conditions in most of Central America justify recourse to revolution. This is especially true of El Salvador. Even the excesses of the despotic, venal Somoza clan in Nicaragua pale in comparison with the brutal, starvation existence imposed on the Salvadoran campesinos and workers by the economic and military elites.

For most of this century the rich of El Salvador—families such as the Quiñonez, the da Solas, the Regelados—have dominated an economy which has systematically reduced the poor to a subhuman existence. In 1979, young officers leagued with democratic revolutionaries and launched a program dedicated to human rights and reform. Their efforts were regularly subverted by Colonel Nicholas Carranza and other high ranking members of the Salvadoran military. When leaders for human dignity and change—men such as Archbishop Oscar Romero and Land Reform Chief Roldolfo Viera—continued their efforts on behalf of the poor, military death squads gunned them down.

The fundamental error of the Reagan foreign policy team has been to hide the fact that death squads and butchery are intrinsic to the regime their policies have helped create. As in Vietnam, this head-in-the-sand approach confuses our own citizens, angers our allies, and does a profound disservice to the peoples we purport to help . . .

For fifty years, El Salvador was ruled by a corrupt and brutal alliance of the rich and the military. The young officers revolt of 1979 attempted to break that alliance. The Carter Administration gave all-out support to the drive for profound change. It rejected the solutions of the extreme right. When the Reagan Administration took office, it reidentified the United States with the military

63

" Let me assure you that I have international terrorism well in hand. "

and economic elites—with disastrous results. It was the Reagan toleration and acceptance of the extreme right which led to the emergence of the National Republican Alliance, ARENA, and the rise of ex-Major Roberto D'Aubuisson.

ARENA

ARENA is a fascist party modeled after the NAZIS and certain revolutionary communist groups. ARENA has a politico-military organization which embraces not only a civilian party structure but also a military arm obedient to the party. The founders and chief supporters of ARENA are rich Salvadoran exiles headquartered in Miami and civilian activists in El Salvador. ARENA's military arm comprises officers and men of the Salvadoran army and Security Forces. Many of its most effective militants in the military are not formal party members.

In the Carter Administration, men such as Vice President Walter Mondale and the two top State Department officers, Cyrus Vance and Warren Christopher, understood that to be effective against the armed, violent, extremist left, the United States had to reject the fascist, murderous right. As a result, my embassy devoted considerable resources to identifying the sources of right wing violence which sought to destroy the working relationship between the Christian Democrats led by José Napoleon

Duarte and the progressive officers led by Colonel Adolfo Majano . . .

The Miami connection

Who are these madmen and how do they operate? The principal figures are six enormously wealthy former landowners who lost great estates in Phase I of the agrarian reform but still have important holdings parcelled out to nephews, cousins, grandsons, etc., that would be taken under Phase II of the land reform; they also have liquid assets and foreign investments which, combined, might be in the range of two to five hundred million dollars. They have always exercised decisive power in this country and cannot believe that their day is over. Their tactics here were simple: co-opt bright people from the middle class, bribe the top military leadership, kill anyone who made trouble. They have continued to pursue these tactics in Miami but on a far greater scale; for instance they have bribed many military officers and politicians here and abroad to serve their interests. But of even more concern is the fact that they organize, fund and direct death squads through their agent, Major Roberto D'Aubuisson. He has been in El Salvador pursuing the strategy of the "six" to destabilize the country and overthrow the Junta, and using their tactics, bombing factories and offices, kidnapping businessmen and now, very likely, murdering the intellectual leadership of land reform. The object is to terrorize those who are still working for a moderate outcome, in or out of the government, and to impose a rightist dictatorship . . .

Roberto D'Aubuisson

The administration of President Carter classified ex-Major Roberto D'Aubuisson, accurately, as a terrorist, a murderer, and a leader of death squads. As ambassador, I denied him access to the United States embassy and succeeded in having him barred from our country.

Shortly after President Reagan took office, this administration overturned this policy and began the process of rehabilitating ex-Major D'Aubuisson. The Reagan administration granted D'Aubuisson a visa to enter the United States, made him an honored guest at our embassy and saw to it that he met regularly with high ranking administration officials and visiting Senators and Congressmen. The legislators were, of course, unaware of the strength of evidence against D'Aubuisson.

Primarily as a result of the Reagan administration's acceptance of D'Aubuisson, his reputation and effectiveness increased. No longer was he a pariah but a legitimate political leader, well and favorably known to the United States embassy. The fortunes of ARENA soared. D'Aubuisson emerged from the March 1982 elections President of the new Constituent Assembly and his country's strong man. In a very real sense, the Reagan administration created Roberto D'Aubuisson the political leader.

Yet from the first days in office the Reagan White House knew—beyond any reasonable doubt—that Roberto D'Aubuisson planned and ordered the assassination of Archbishop Oscar Arnulfo Romero. In mid-November of 1980, a particularly brave and resourceful American diplomat made contact with a Salvadoran military officer who had participated in the plot to kill Archbishop Romero. This officer was present at the March 22nd meeting which resulted in the death of Archbishop Romero on March 24.

According to this eyewitness account, Roberto D'Aubuisson

U.S. Participation In Death Squads

Early in the 1960s, during the Kennedy Administration, agents of the U.S. Government in El Salvador set up two official security organizations that killed thousands of peasants and suspected leftists over the next fifteen years. These organizations, guided by American operatives, developed into the paramilitary apparatus that came to be known as the Salvadoran Death Squads.

Today, even as the Reagan Administration publicly condemns the Death Squads, the CIA—in violation of U.S. law—continues to provide training, support, and intelligence to security forces directly involved in Death Squad activity.

Interviews with dozens of current and former Salvadoran officers, civilians, and official American sources disclose a pattern of sustained U.S. participation in building and managing the Salvadoran security apparatus that relies on Death Squad assassinations as its principal means of enforcement.

Allan Nairn, *The Progressive*, May, 1984.

summoned a group of about twelve men to a safe house, presided over the meeting, announced the decision to assassinate the Archbishop and supervised the drawing of lots for the "honor" of carrying out the plot. The Salvadoran officer informant was disappointed that the luck of the draw had not favored him. He gave bullets from his gun to the officer selected in order that he might participate vicariously in the murder of the Archbishop.

The officer who "won" the lottery was Lt. Francisco Amaya Rosa, a D'Aubuisson intimate. Amaya Rosa chose a military hanger-on and sharpshooter named Walter Antonio Alvarez to fire the single bullet which ended the life of Archbishop Romero as he said Mass in the orphanage of the Good Shephard . . .

The road to peace—Negotiations

In my judgment, as long as we continue military aid to the present military leadership of El Salvador, they will never permit negotiations.

It does not matter who is president. As long as the Salvadoran military is controlled by men who collaborate with ARENA in its campaign of wholesale torture and murder, no negotiations are possible . . .

The only way to defeat the extreme left is to reject the extreme right. What we face in Central America is primarily a political challenge, and only marginally a military threat. The task is not, as the Kissinger commission imagines, to defeat the revolutionaries on the battlefield. The challenge is to prevent the Soviet Union and Cuba from capturing the forces of change. The day the young leaders of Central America see Communist countries as their only arsenal for political and logistical support for throwing off bloody dictatorship is the day our security will truly be in jeopardy.

The United States must change its policy and begin to work for peace in Central America. El Salvador is the key. Let us join with democratic partners in Latin America and apply the Costa Rican model to El Salvador. Working through the Contadora countries, negotiators would seek an agreement in which the Salvadoran military and the revolutionaries would ratify a cease-fire and the presence of an Inter-American peacekeeping force. Both the military and the revolutionaries would then disband, and after two years of peace and order, democratic elections would take place. In the post-election period a small national police force could gradually take over and replace the peacekeeping mission. As in Costa Rica, the military would be permanently abolished and political liberties guaranteed by civilian rule.

In order to bring us closer to this goal, tough action by Congress is necessary. Such action should include:

1. A stipulation that no further military aid shall go to El Salvador unless the Government of El Salvador carries out, in the words of the Kissinger Commission, "vigorous action against those guilty of crimes and the prosecution to the extent possible, of past offenders"; and the United States government carries out "serious sanctions, including the denial of visas [and] deportation" of US-based Salvadorans involved in death squad activities;

2. A stipulation that Congress, not the President, will make this determination prior to allocating any further funds to El Salvador . . .

The Congress should support negotiations by conditioning further military aid to El Salvador upon serious negotiations by both sides.

10

THE COUNTERPOINT

PROMOTING DEMOCRATIC PLURALISM

National Bipartisan Commission on Central America

President Reagan commissioned and appointed what he called a bipartisan commission to study the problem of Central America and make policy recommendations to the Congress. Henry Kissinger, the chief foreign policy advisor to President Nixon, served as chairman of this commission.

Points To Consider

1. What is the relationship between human rights abuses and military aid?
2. What is the relationship between U.S. national security and human rights?
3. Why should military and economic aid to Central American governments be increased?
4. Should any strings be attached to military aid?

Excerpted from the Report of the National Bipartisan Commission on Central America, 1984.

We have stressed the need to make American development assistance strictly conditional on rapid progress towards democratic pluralism and respect for human rights.

The question of the relationship between military aid and human rights abuses is both extremely difficult and extremely important. It involves the potential clash of two basic U.S. objectives. On the one hand, we seek to promote justice and find it repugnant to support forces that violate—or tolerate violation of—fundamental U.S. values. On the other hand, we are engaged in El Salvador and Central America because we are serving fundamental U.S. interests that transcend any particular government.

Our approach must therefore embrace, and pursue, both objectives simultaneously. Clearly, sustained public and international support rests heavily on our success in harmonizing our dual goals. Against this background, we have stressed the need to make American development assistance strictly conditional on rapid progress towards democratic pluralism and respect for human rights, as well as economic performance. Respect for human rights is also of great importance to improved security in Central America, as well as to the self-respect of the United States. We recognize, however, that how the problem is addressed in this regard is vital because Central America is crucial to our national security.

Twin objectives

While the objectives of security and human rights are sometimes counterposed against each other, they are actually closely related. Without adequate military aid, Salvadoran forces would not be able to carry out the modern counter-insurgency tactics that would help keep civilian losses to a minimum. Were military aid to be cut off, it would open the way for the triumph of the guerrillas, an eventuality that no one concerned about the well-being of the Salvadoran people can accept with equanimity. Such a development would be unacceptable from the standpoint of both human rights and security.

The Commission believes that vigorous, concurrent policies on both the military and human rights fronts are needed to break out of the demoralizing cycle of deterioration on the one hand and abuses on the other. We believe policies of increased aid and increased pressure to safeguard human rights would improve security and justice. A slackening on one front would un-

70

CENTRAL AMERICA

dermine our objective on the other. El Salvador must succeed on both or it will not succeed on either.

The United States Government has a right to demand certain minimum standards of respect for human rights as a condition for providing military aid to any country.

With respect to El Salvador, military aid should, through legislation requiring periodic reports, be made contingent upon demonstrated progress toward free elections; freedom of association; the establishment of the rule of law and an effective judicial system; and the termination of the activities of the so-called death squads, as well as vigorous action against those guilty of crimes and the prosecution to the extent possible of past offenders. These conditions should be seriously enforced.

Implementation of this approach would be greatly facilitated through the device of an independent monitoring body, such as the Central American Development Organization.

As an additional measure, the United States should impose sanctions, including the denial of visas, deportation, and the investigation of financial dealings, against foreign nationals in the United States who are connected with death-squad activities in El Salvador or anywhere else.

It is the Commission's judgment that the same policy approach should be employed in the case of Guatemala. The existing human rights situation there is unacceptable and the security could become critical. Although the insurgency in Guatemala has been contained for the time being at a relatively low level, military assistance could become necessary. Military aid and military sales should be authorized if Guatemala meets the human rights conditions described in this chapter. In terms of regional and U.S. security interests, Guatemala, with its strategic position on the Mexican border, the largest population in the Central American area and the most important economy, is obviously a pivotal country.

Why Marxism Is Evil

So what is to be done? Marxism is not an evil because it installs a socialist economy. If a nation wishes to thwart its own economic growth and permanently impoverish itself, that is its own business . . .

Marxism is an evil because its foreign policy *cannot* be isolationist. Marxism is a quasi-religion. Its essence is a vision of power in history, power necessarily flowing toward the police and the military might of Marxist states. Marxist states do not, and cannot, believe in international laissez-faire. Believing Marxists acquire a moral obligation to carry Marxism, by force, to all the nations.

Michael Novak, National Review, *1983*

Conclusion

The Commission has concluded that the security interests of the United States are importantly engaged in Central America; that these interests require a significantly larger program of military assistance, as well as greatly expanded support for economic growth and social reform; that there must be an end to the massive violation of human rights if security is to be achieved in Central America; and that external support for the insurgency must be neutralized for the same purpose.

The deterioration in Central America has been such that we cannot afford paralysis in defending our national interests and in achieving our national purposes. The fact that such paralysis resulted from the lack of a national consensus on foreign policy in the United States would not mitigate the consequences of failure. We believe that a consensus is possible, and must be achieved, on an issue of such importance to the national security of the United States.

We would hope, moreover, that a clear U.S. commitment to such a course would itself improve the prospects for successful negotiations—so that arms would support diplomacy rather than supplant it.

STOP THE MILITARY AID

The People Newspaper

The People *is the official publication of the Socialist Labor Party headquartered in Palo Alto, California. The following statement deals with the relationship between military aid to El Salvador and human rights violations. An end to military aid is advocated.*

Points To Consider

1. How is the government in El Salvador described?
2. What is the goal of the U.S. and Salvadoran governments?
3. What is the human rights record of El Salvador's government?
4. Why should military support for El Salvador be ended?

"No Human Rights in El Salvador," *The People*, April 14, 1984, p. 9.

As the record amply testifies, the U.S. government has no compunctions about supporting a regime that is ruthlessly violating human rights.

The current debate about whether U.S. military aid to El Salvador should be tied to improvements in human rights is a sham. For the facts show that the Salvadoran regime that the U.S. government supports is the principal perpetrator of the human-rights violations—such as murder—that are a daily occurrence in El Salvador.

Yet that brutal regime is not quite a puppet government. It is largely supported by, and beholden to the native large landholding capitalists. This is a source of conflict between the U.S. government and elements of the regime over strategy and tactics.

However, since the military coup of 1979, the United States has been the main supporter of the regime, the principal source of its arms and military training. Last year it funded well over 80 percent of the Salvadoran government's military budget and a high percentage of its other operations as well. Without continued U.S. backing, the present regime would crumble within months. This underscores the fact that the United States is interfering in El Salvador's internal affairs and denying the Salvadoran people their right to determine their own destiny.

A common goal

The U.S. and Salvadoran governments have the same basic goal. That goal is to destroy the rebel movement, pacify the worker-peasant majority, and bring the country under effective government control so that U.S. and Salvadoran capitalists can return to "business as usual"—ruthlessly exploiting the workers and the peasants for maximum profit.

Toward that end, the Salvadoran military regime and its death squads are using brutal repression, indiscriminately massacring workers and peasants on the mere suspicion that they might be rebels or rebel supporters.

Just as U.S. military officers did in Vietnam, Salvadoran officers have admitted that they have difficulty determining who is or is not a rebel—thereby seeking to justify indiscriminate slaughter. Indeed, last fall, rebels tape recorded a Salvadoran officer giving an order to bomb a village, saying "anyone who is not a soldier is an enemy."

Despite the administration's big show of trying to crack down on the Salvadoran death squads, the main human rights violator

Military Aid

Medical Aid

remains the Salvadoran regime itself. Its national police and military forces murdered over 5,000 civilians in 1983, and torture, "disappearances," and numerous other forms of intimidation

75

Under the Jackboot

Each dawn, mutilated bodies of civilians appear in ditches to remind the poor of the barbaric system under which they live—under the jackboot of the Salvadoran military. No wonder the revolutionaries move among the people like fish through the sea.

Robert White, Ambassador to El Salvador during the Carter administration, 1983

and repression are routine. Many more civilians were murdered by roving right-wing death squads composed largely of off-duty soldiers.

The U.S. and human rights

As the record amply testifies, the U.S. government has no compunctions about supporting a regime that is ruthlessly violating human rights. But it is concerned with its *image* as a defender of freedom and democracy. With so much international and domestic attention now focused on El Salvador, the United States is trying hard to maintain the facade that it is working to improve the human rights situation there.

Thus it is sending contradictory messages to its Salvadoran partner; wipe out the rebels, but tone down the slaughter and repression of their worker and peasant supporters.

The Salvadoran military generally has failed to do either, and its more extreme right factions aren't even inclined to try to tone down the slaughter. These factions are banking on the conviction that the United States will not abandon the Salvadoran regime no matter what it does—and that premise appears to be correct . . .

Salvadoran 'progress'

It has recently come to light that the U.S. reports of a gradual decline in civilian deaths caused by government forces and the death squads, have been based on figures that come from El Salvador's newspapers, which in turn get their figures from the Salvadoran government.

The Salvadoran government does not count the deaths of civilians who it *believes* were rebel supporters. Thus, while the U.S. government has been claiming that the killings of civilians have been declining to about 100 a month, figures compiled from firsthand testimony show an increase over the last half of 1983—to over 400 murders a month.

Similarly, the administration has repeatedly proclaimed progress in the Salvadoran land-reform program. Yet not only has that program been inadequate and riddled with loopholes from the start, it has been further gutted by legislative modifications, delays, corruption, forcible eviction of peasants, and other reversals.

For example, the Salvadoran assembly voted to exempt 95 percent of the land under cultivation from the "land to the tiller" program, and an estimated 15,000 families were evicted at gunpoint from land they had received under the program. Yet on July 20, the Reagan administration simply asserted that "agrarian reform has continued to move ahead" in "certifying" progress once again . . .

Congress has been "warning" the Salvadoran regime and "threatening" to revoke its support for a good three years now, but the bloodshed continues unabated. In a rather candid remark

---

U.S. Army Teaches Torture Techniques

An El Salvadoran refugee given sanctuary by a Minnetonka church has disclosed that he raped a woman and beat and tortured prisoners many times while a member of his country's treasury police . . .

In an interview with the Minneapolis Star and Tribune last week, he acknowledged that he personally tortured prisoners with techniques he said he was taught by U.S. Army Green Berets.

"I tortured them in order to interrogate them," he said. "I beat persons many times". . .

• Raped a woman on a public street, knowing he would not be punished because of his membership in the treasury police, a branch of the Salvadoran national security forces.

• Applied electric shocks to people he interrogated, tore off their skin . . .

Randy Furst, Minneapolis Star and Tribune, 1984

during the recent congressional debate on aid to El Salvador, Sen. Patrick Leahy (D-Vt.) put the debate in perspective: "Here we are saying how concerned we are, and yet we are giving them money all over again. Let's not kid ourselves into thinking that it's going to make a single change."

Maintaining U.S. domination

The failure of Congress to take decisive action to cut off military aid to the brutal El Salvador regime reflects its support for the basic U.S. goal of maintaining domination of that country. Even the liberal congressional critics of the administration don't dispute that basic goal. They simply favor trying to accomplish it through means such as a "negotiated settlement."

They favor that course for tactical, pragmatic reasons. As Rep. David Obey (D-Wis.) put it, "power sharing is better than in the end losing it all."

But liberal critics of the administration's policies don't go so far as to say that the United States has no right at all to interfere in Salvadoran affairs. None of them stand up for the right of the Salvadoran people to be completely free of U.S. imperialism if they so choose.

For all their seeming concern about human rights, both liberal and conservative wings of the U.S. government continue to support the existing Salvadoran regime precisely because it is working to suppress the anti-imperialist struggle of El Salvador's workers and peasants. If there is to be progress in human rights in El Salvador, it won't come from the U.S. government, but from the actions of both the U.S. and the Salvadoran working classes.

12

THE COUNTERPOINT

MILITARY AID SHOULD BE INCREASED

Melvyn Krauss

Dr. Melvyn Krauss is a professor of economics at New York University and senior fellow at the Hoover Institution, a conservative think tank at Stanford University. The following statement was excerpted from testimony by Dr. Krauss before the Senate Foreign Relations Committee.

Points To Consider

1. How are the objectives of U.S. policy in Central America defined?
2. What is the most important objective?
3. How important is military aid?
4. Why should increased military aid not be made conditional on improvement in human rights?

Excerpted from testimony by Melvyn Krauss before the Senate Foreign Relations Committee, 1984.

The United States has clear interests in Central America. These are to promote *political democracy* and *economic prosperity*. Attainment of these two objectives is important both for humanitarian and U.S. national security reasons.

We should not underestimate the enormity of this task. Political democracy, in particular, is like a gem valued both for its beauty and scarcity. In truth, there are very few examples of working democracies in the poorer countries . . .

We must recognize the long-term nature of this objective and that there is a reasonable chance of failure. To insure ourselves in case of failure, the economic role that government plays in Central American societies should be scaled down. Political democracy, after all, refers to the political process, not the market system. The more things done through the market system, and the less through the political process, the less relevant will be the failure to achieve political democracy, at least in a relatively short time. For example, popular control over the political process is much more important in a socialist society where government distributes 90 percent of the national income than in a capitalistic society where it distributes 10 percent. There is simply more at stake in politics when economic life is highly politicized.

Government's economic role

This is not to argue, of course, that political democracy is not a worthwhile objective. It most certainly is. Only that we should be realistic as to our prospects for achieving it in regions of the world where traditions have run in opposite directions.

Happily, reducing the role that government plays in the nation's economic life also is an indispensable condition for promoting economic prosperity in poorer countries. In comparing East Germany with West Germany, North Korea with South Korea, Red China with Nationalist China, Finland with the Soviet Union and the Ivory Coast with Ghana, it is always the country with big government that has produced continuing poverty for its citizens, while that with small government has produced economic prosperity.

The single most prosperous region of the third world during the past quarter century has been the Pacific Basin area. And the countries of this area, by and large, have allowed government to play a small role in their economic lives.

One conclusion, therefore, is inescapable: that the United States must use its influence in Central America to reduce the role that Central American governments play in their society's economic life. We must promote the privatization of the Central American economies and discourage their socialization. We should use the Pacific basin area as a model . . .

Small land owners in El Salvador

The way the U.S. can help privatize the economies of Central America is to promote political stability there. One does not have to be a professional economist to understand that political stability is a necessary condition for economic prosperity; without it, businessmen will not invest, lenders will not lend and foreign capital will not flow in. The sad truth is that as long as the central American economies are externally threatened by Soviet-sponsored aggression, economic progress will not be possible.

A military solution

Some in this country argue for a "military solution" and others for an "economic solution" to Central American problems as if the two were competitors, not partners. This couldn't be further from the truth. A "military solution " is an essential precondition for an "economic solution". And the "economic solution" is what ultimately justifies the use of military force. Because economic progress in Central America is imperative for our long-run national security interests—and for humanitarian reasons as well—the United States must help governments in this region defend themselves against external aggression.

I thus would like to associate myself with those recommendations of the Report of the National Bipartisan Commission on Central America that call for increased levels of military support for the governments of El Salvador, Honduras and other Central American countries.

In summation, I agree with the Commission's findings that U.S. interests in Central America are vital. It is one thing to have hostile governments thousands of miles from our shores; another to have them on our front doorstep.

Increased military assistance to the area can provide the political stability essential for economic development. Decreased economic aid will help shrink the economic role government plays and thus privatize the economy. If our government really is sincere in its desire to render economic assistance to our Central American neighbors, it should give their exports *unlimited* and *unconditional* access to U.S. markets. That's the kind of help that would do the people—and not just the ruling elites in these countries—a lot of good.

Human rights

Finally, *increased military assistance should not be made conditional on improvements in human rights.* No matter how important the concept may be to us, it is degrading for a great power such as the United States to have to impose human rights conditions on its military assistance. It implies this country somehow is not in control (and that the recipient countries are out of control). This is not the case, as I understand it. And there would appear to be no acceptable reason why the U.S. should give this false impression to the rest of the world.

Moreover, realistic human rights conditions are hard to define. Operationally, they are difficult to impose without being either irrelevant (too easily met) or, what is more likely, too stringent in which case our friends have to fight with one hand tied behind their backs while friends of the Soviets do not.

Eradicate The Guerrillas

There is a war on in Central America. As long as there is a war on, there will be economic disruption and social suffering. We cannot expect that the Salvadorans can divide their energies between social and political reforms while trying to win a war at the same time.

The first step should be the eradication of the guerrilla movement; only after that can we expect progress towards a stable society.

Senator Jesse Helms, 1984

WHAT IS ETHNOCENTRIC BIAS?

This activity may be used as an individualized study guide for students in libraries and resource centers or as a discussion catalyst in small group and classroom discussions.

Many readers are unaware that written material usually expresses an opinion or bias. The skill to read with insight and understanding requires the ability to detect different kinds of bias. Political bias, race bias, sex bias, ethnocentric bias and religious bias are five basic kinds of opinions expressed in editorials and literature that attempt to persuade. This activity will focus on ethnocentric bias defined in the glossary below.

FIVE KINDS OF EDITORIAL OPINION OR BIAS

*sex bias—the expression of dislike for and/or feeling of superiority over a person because of gender or sexual preference

*race bias—the expression of dislike for and/or feeling of superiority over a racial group

*ethnocentric bias—the expression of a belief that one's own group, race, religion, culture or nation is superior. Ethnocentric persons judge others by their own standards and values

*political bias—the expression of opinions and attitudes about government related issues on the local, state or international level

*religious bias—the expression of a religious belief or attitude

Guidelines

Read through the following statements and decide which ones represent ethnocentric opinions or bias. Evaluate each statement by using the method indicated.
Place the letter (E) in front of any sentence that reflects ethnocentric opinion or bias.
Place the letter (N) in front of any sentence that does not reflect ethnocentric opinion or bias.
Place the letter (S) in front of any sentence that you are not sure about.

83

___ 1. In today's world, it is important to have universal compulsory military training.

___ 2. The draft should be abolished.

___ 3. Right-wing death squads are El Salvador's most serious internal threat.

___ 4. Left-wing death squads are El Salvador's most serious internal threat.

___ 5. Bad feelings toward the United States by other nations are largely caused by envy.

___ 6. The appeal of communism is gained largely through programs of social and economic equality.

___ 7. Whatever its faults, the United States has a better way of life than any nation in the world.

___ 8. Christianity is the religion that makes America a strong and prosperous nation.

___ 9. The United States must help its allies defeat communism all over the world.

___ 10. The American military is defending American business interests around the world, not democracy and freedom.

___ 11. The United States is a better country to live in than the Soviet Union.

___ 12. We should be willing to fight for our country whether it is right or wrong.

___ 13. It is obvious that other nations are often conspiring against the United States.

___ 14. Capitalist nations can usually be trusted more than socialist countries.

___ 15. The main problem with American foreign policy today is that there is too much reliance on military force.

Other Activities

1. Try to locate examples of ethnocentric statements in this or other publications.

2. Make up one statement that would be an example of each of the following: **sex bias, race bias, political opinion or bias, and religious bias.**

3. See if you can locate any factual statements in the fifteen items listed above.

CHAPTER 4

CENTRAL AMERICAN REFUGEES: THE FLIGHT FROM TERROR

13

IDEAS IN CONFLICT

PROVIDING AN AMERICAN SANCTUARY

Patrick A. Taran

This article was excerpted from an article in the **Refugees and Human Rights Newsletter** *for the Church World Service Immigration and Refugee Program. The article is distributed by the Inter-Religious Task Force on El Salvador and Central America, 475 Riverside Drive, Room 633, New York, N.Y. 10155.*

Points To Consider

1. What are the roots of the Exodus in El Salvador?
2. How many refugees have fled El Salvador and Guatemala?
3. What should be the U.S. policy toward Central American refugees?
4. How are the churches responding?
5. Why does Nicaragua present the brightest prospect for dealing with refugees and displaced persons?

Patrick A. Taran, **Refugees and Human Rights Newsletter**, Summer, 1983.

To recognize that refugees are fleeing in large numbers from countries whose governments the U.S. supports might well call into question that support.

The conflicts in Central America are driving a steady stream of stunned and terrorized refugees to countries throughout the region and into the United States. It is hard for most Americans to hear the stories these refugees tell, for they are stories about the violence convulsing their homelands—a violence in which the barbaric has become commonplace. The U.S. government refuses to accept these persons as refugees. To do so would imply tacit recognition, at the very least, that the governments of the countries from which they are fleeing—governments which the U.S. supports—are unable or unwilling to guarantee the safety of their citizens. But many congregations across the country are acting in different ways to help and protect these refugees.

The roots of the exodus in El Salvador

Since early 1980, international observers have characterized the situation in El Salvador as one of widespread civil warfare. Human rights violations have been extremely high, with most sources indicating at least 40,000 civilian deaths since the beginning of 1980.

Until late 1979, El Salvador had been ruled by the world's longest succession of dictatorial military regimes. In 1979, a coup brought to power a civil-military junta which was unable to find a middle ground between the majority of the population which demanded changes and the powerful minority which opposed even the most minimal reforms. The situation rapidly deteriorated into a state of civil warfare as the government embarked on what one church spokesperson described as a "war of extermination against the civilian populace," and the opposition took up arms as a last resort in its struggle for social justice.

Tens of thousands of people are now displaced in El Salvador. None feel safe in the atmosphere of pervasive violence. Refugee camps are often raided by paramilitary bands looking for "subversives." Church and humanitarian relief workers have been killed or harassed. Those displaced in rebel-held areas have been bombed and attacked by government troops. Many church people are among those who have been forced to leave their homes and flee.

At least a half million more Salvadorans have fled the country altogether. The United Nations High Commissioner for Refugees

U.S. activist translates statement of Salvadoran refugee seeking sanctuary at Luther Place Church in Washington.

(UNHCR) and voluntary relief agencies estimate that some 300,000 Salvadoran refugees are spread across Central America and Mexico.

The Guatemalan parallel

The situation in Guatemala is disturbingly similar to that in El Salvador. The extreme disparity between the wealth of a tiny majority and the abject misery of a peasant majority has generated explosive tensions. In the face of severe government repression to maintain the status quo, armed opposition developed. Large-scale military offensives against guerrilla activity in the countryside have been accompanied by atrocities—described by some observers as "genocidal"—against civilian peasants. The destruction of entire villages and massacre of their inhabitants, most of whom are Indians, has been documented by the National Council of Churches, Amnesty International and other outside observers.

As a result of these upheavals, well over half a million of Guatemala's eight million people are displaced inside that country, according to estimates by Guatemala's Roman Catholic bishops. Estimates of the number of Guatemalans who have fled into neighboring Mexico range upwards of 100,000. Refugees in camps near the border live in fear of deadly raids from Guatemalan territory.

Nicaragua

Counterrevolutionary or *contra* military attacks against Nicaragua left more than 1,000 Nicaraguans dead in 1983. The *contra* operations staged from base camps in Honduras and Costa Rica, financed by the CIA, have forced the displacement or relocation of over 90,000 Nicaraguans away from homes and lands in the border areas under frequent attack. The threat of attack on Miskito indigenous communities along the border in Eastern Nicaragua prompted the government to relocate some 11,000 Miskitos in 1981. At the same time, several thousand Miskitos crossed over the river border into Honduras.

Precarious Refuge in the Region

The situation faced by most refugees fleeing their homelands to other countries in the region has been bleak. El Salvadorans who fled to Honduras have been attacked by pursuing troops and on several occasions by Honduran troops as well. Those who attempted to resettle near the border were subjected to attacks and kidnappings by Salvadoran military and paramilitary bands from across the border. In the last year, most were summarily relocated away from the border, ostensibly for their own protection. There have also been attacks against Guatemalan refugees in the El Tesoro camp in northern Honduras.

The treatment of Salvadoran and Guatemalan refugees in Honduras differs sharply from that given the refugees who have left Nicaragua. The nearly 20,000 Miskitos are being allowed to resettle on agricultural land, and 2,000 other Nicaraguans live in towns and have relative freedom of movement. The 19,000 Salvadoran and 550 Guatemalan refugees are confined to camp sites and are kept under strict military surveillance. Nicaraguan refugees in Honduras, both Miskito Indians and former members of the dictator Somoza's National Guard, are widely reported to be recruited and trained for anti-government raids into Nicaragua.

The attitude of the Mexican government has become increasingly hostile towards Central American refugees whom it sees increasingly as a threat to Mexican security and stability and for whom it has few resources. In 1982, UNHCR estimated that some 120,000 Salvadoran refugees were in Mexico. More than 100,000 Guatemalans are believed to have sought haven there, too. Nongovernmental agencies are not permitted to work or provide aid directly to these refugees.

Nicaragua presents the brightest panorama for refugees and displaced persons. Most of the some 22,000 Salvadoran refugees and the 90,000 internally displaced there have been given

lands to farm and resources to build communities and agricultural cooperatives.

No haven in the United States

At least 250,000 Salvadorans and Guatemalans have arrived in
the U.S. in the last four years. Three very compelling motiva-
tions draw many of those forced to flee their homelands. Refuge
and survival in neighboring lands, including Mexico, is all but
unavailable and impossible. Many of those who come have family and/or friends already in this country. And they come because this is the United States, known as the land of opportunity, or at least where there is a job and there isn't generalized
persecution. Central American refugees continue to arrive by the
thousands each month and will continue to do so as conditions
deteriorate further in Central America.

The official U.S. response to these Central Americans seeking
haven here has been to characterize them as economically moti-
vated illegal immigrants, and to apprehend and deport or expel
them back to their homelands. In late 1983, deportations and ex-
pulsions of Salvadorans numbered some 400 to 500 per month.
While the fate of most has not been investigated, there are several well-documented cases of persons who were killed after
being returned to El Salvador from the U.S.

Individual political asylum status has simply not been available for Salvadorans and Guatemalans. Until recently, many of
those apprehended by the U.S. Immigration and Naturalization
Service (INS) were not informed that there is such a status and
that they had a right to apply for it. Thousands of Central Americans have been denied access to lawyers or legal information
and pressured and coerced into waiving rights and agreeing to
depart "voluntarily" from the U.S. While abuses diminished after
a U.S. District Court in California ordered a halt to such practices
in mid-1982, lawyers and church activists working on behalf of
detainees continue to report numerous difficulties in aiding Central Americans held by INS.

Few of the Central Americans who do apply are granted political asylum. Of the more than 22,000 Salvadorans who applied
for asylum in the last three years, only some 1,100 cases have
been decided. As of September, 1983 only 74 were granted asylum. The U.S. government has also refused, despite many
Congressional, church and public appeals, to apply an available
administrative measure called Extended Voluntary Departure status to temporarily suspend deportations of Salvadorans and
Guatemalans until the violence subsides in their homelands.

Sanctuary

Over 92 churches in some 45 communities throughout the country have taken the bold step of offering "sanctuary" to Central American refugees, publicly declaring that they take into the care, protection and sanctuary of the church building undocumented refugees otherwise threatened with apprehension by U.S. immigration authorities and likely deportation or expulsion back to their homelands.

By offering sanctuary in probable violation of federal immigration law, these churches have publicly challenged the morality and legality of current government policy of returning refugees to homelands where persecution is likely. In doing so, the sanctuary movement has played a significant role in making the plight of the victims of the conflict in Central America an issue of national concern and debate.

The fundamental issues

As the church responses have highlighted, U.S. political and economic policies toward Central America are bound up with the root causes forcing refugees to flee those same countries. The practice of denying haven to Salvadorans and Guatemalans arriving in this country appears to be consistent with official support for the regimes governing their homelands. To recognize these people as bona fide refugees would be, at the very least, tacit recognition that those governments are unable or unwilling to guarantee the security of their citizens. Such recognition would draw increasing attention to the government responsibility for widescale atrocities and civilian deaths in El Salvador and Guatemala. And to recognize that refugees are fleeing in large numbers from countries whose governments the U.S. supports might well call into question that support.

Most Central American refugees insist that they want to go home, when the violence ends. The establishment of a temporary legal status for these refugees means that while the warfare continues, they can remain here without fear of being forcibly repatriated.

PREVENTING A FLOOD OF REFUGEES

Ronald S. Godwin

Dr. Ronald S. Godwin is a frequent contributor to the Moral Majority Report, the official national publication of the Moral Majority. The Moral Majority defines itself as a political organization attempting to bring traditional American religious and conservative values back into the political area. They support political candidates and programs in the republican and democratic parties. They are concerned with the issues of national defense, gay rights, pornography, voluntary prayer in schools, abortion on demand and others.

Points To Consider

1. If we do not help our Latin neighbors now, what will happen?
2. What kind of help is advocated?
3. What will it take to solve the problem of refugees?
4. How did columnist Pat Buchanan describe the problem?

Dr. Ronald S. Godwin, "Congress Must Act Now to Prevent Flood of Central American Refugees to U.S., **Moral Majority Report**, June, 1983, p. 8.

Do we have the force of will to deal with Congress and the Marxist sympathizers in the national media, or will we soon have to confront refugees pouring northward on the Pan American Highway?

The U.S. Catholic Bishops and Congressional liberals are at it again: playing politics with defense policies. But this time they aren't trying to give away someone else's right to freedom and survival. This time they threaten America's very survival with their latest brew of liberal idealism and partisan politics. And, finally, this time they may have gone too far or have come too close—for large numbers of even their most loyal constituents.

House liberals aid Marxists

While the Bishops rush in with moral judgments, where even experts fear to tread, certain Congressmen continue to play their own deadly partisan game of politics with Central America. And, like the Bishops, this time they aren't just playing God with the lives of people on the other side of the world. This time they are aiding Marxists within walking distance of the Texas border.

Sen. Jesse Helms, R-N.C., has repeatedly warned his Senate colleagues about the "walking distance" aspect of the Central American crisis. Plainly stated, we either help our Latin neighbors now where they live or help them later as refugees in south Texas. If the Marxist terrorists win in Central America, America will reel under a flood of refugees and the American public knows this—whether or not some members of Congress want to admit it.

The small countries between Mexico and Panama are connected to the United States by a land bridge. If the citizens of these countries flee their homeland, they will flee northward. If they do flee our way, we will have reaped what we have sown for the past several decades.

More aid needed

For all too long, the United States has largely ignored these countries. We didn't mind the dictators, the grinding poverty, the generalized inhumanity of those in power toward those out of power, so long as those in power were friendly toward America. We have been far less than good neighbors for all too long. And now, in a too little, too late move, our country has belatedly stepped in with some half-hearted help.

93

Salvadoran refugees.

"Half-hearted help" is too kind, really, to accurately describe what the United States is doing, particularly in El Salvador. Every time President Reagan attempts to do more certain key Congressmen gut the appropriation.

U.S. Ambassador to the United Nations, Jeane Kirkpatrick, states flatly there are those in Congress who would like to see El Salvador and other Central American countries come under the rule of the Marxists.

Regardless of their motivation, clearly a hard-core group in Congress intends to do everything in their power to neutralize America's support for the people of El Salvador. And Moral Majority readers had better realize the deadly danger such Congressional action presents the United States.

As columnist Pat Buchanan said recently, "We have 6000 troops in distant West Berlin, 30,000 troops in South Korea, 100,000 being trained for the Rapid Deployment Force to engage

94

the Soviets on the Persian Gulf, 300,000 assigned to NATO. How credible is all this force if the United States proves militarily incapable of blocking a few thousand guerrillas from establishing half a dozen Cubas on the doorstep of the United States?"

Military victory

The United States has waited dangerously long before deciding Central America is worth saving. At this late date, it will take a clear military victory on the volcanic slopes of El Salvador for that country to survive. Do we have the force of will to deal with Congress and the Marxist sympathizers in the national media, or will we soon have to confront refugees pouring northward on the Pan American Highway?

REFUGEES FLEE POLITICAL TERROR

Daniel P. Sheehan

Daniel P. Sheehan is an attorney for the Sanctuary Defense Fund established by the Christic Institute. This Fund helps defend in the courts those American citizens charged with "illegally" helping political refugees from Central America and helps keep these refugees from being sent back to their own countries where they fear torture and murder.

Points To Consider

1. Why does the sanctuary movement exist?
2. Why are members of the movement being arrested by government authorities?
3. What proof does the author cite to indicate that returning refugees face torture and murder in Central America?
4. What is the underground railroad?

Excerpted from a position paper by Daniel P. Sheehan, Sanctuary Defense Fund of the Christic Institute, 1984.

Shall the guest in our house be sent away to certain death?

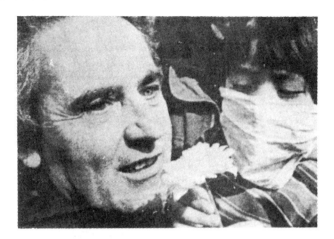

Why is this child wearing a mask?

Quite simply, to prevent his being identified and murdered in cold blood if the U.S. Executive Department succeeds in forcing him and his family to go back to certain death in their tortured homeland of Guatemala.

For the moment he is safe—he and his family sheltered in a benedictine Monastery in Vermont where Brother John is the Prior.

This monastery is just one of more than a hundred churches, religious homes and other sanctuaries that are part of an extraordinary new movement that springs from the very heart and spiritual roots of our American heritage of freedom and justice.

It is the **Sanctuary Movement** in which American religious leaders of many denominations and thousands of private individuals have joined to reestablish a principle that goes back to the dawn of civilization—

That the guest in our house shall not be sent away to certain death.

Unless we act now, at least three such guests (one an 18-month old baby) will be sent away—and two religious workers may go to jail for 15 years for helping them. Please let me tell you what happened.

Just before dawn on February 17, 1984, on a deserted Texas highway, 3 Americans and 3 Salvadorans were arrested.

The three Americans were Stacey Merkt, a Catholic lay worker, Sister Dianne Muhlenkamp, and a reporter for the Dallas Times-Herald. Stacy was working for a home—sponsored by the

97

"Take your tired, your poor, your huddled masses . . ."

By David Seavey, USA TODAY

Reprinted with permission of *USA Today.*

Catholic diocese of Brownsville—which gives hospitality to Central American refugees fleeing for their lives. Stacey, the only Sanctuary worker in the car, has now been charged with transporting illegal aliens.

Who were these three dangerous aliens this religious worker was "illegally" transporting?

Mauricio Valle, 23, and Brenda Sanchez-Galan, 19, fled El Salvador in fear for their lives. They swam across the Rio Grande with Bessie, Brenda's 18-month-old daughter, to enter this country. With the church's assistance, they were bound for San Antonio, Texas, to receive legal counseling. Both had worked for Green Cross, a non-partisan organization like the American Red Cross which gives medical care to refugees. The organization was a target of a campaign of terror and violence by the Salvadoran military. Brenda had watched as a co-worker was brutally killed in a public courtyard and the fetus in her womb mutilated. Lutheran churchworkers advised her that she too would probably be killed and helped her out of the country.

Mauricio's father, who worked with the Lutheran church in El Salvador, had nursed a wounded man in 1979 whom the military declared to be a subversive. As a result, the military issued death threats against him, his daughter and his son. The father and daughter committed suicide. Mauricio escaped after being kidnapped by the Death Squads and threatened with death.

Central American policies

President Reagan's Central American policies are the cause of the flow of refugees into this country. He has continued to support the repressive governments of El Salvador and Guatemala without regard to human rights violations. He is advocating a military solution to the region's problems, pouring out millions of dollars in military aid to governments for use against their own people.

Salvadoran refugees who flee to the United States have become an acute political embarrassment as they tell of murders committed by military units armed and trained by the U.S. government. It's not surprising that—contrary to the clear intent of Congress—the Reagan Administration has classified Salvadorans as economic rather than political refugees. **As such, they are not eligible for asylum and are deported back to their country, where their lives are in great danger.**

But most Americans do not think in terms of warlike solutions. They do not support governments built on Death Squads that murder their own people by the thousands.

Nor will most Americans turn away families fleeing for their lives and send them back to certain death—death even for 18-month-old Bessie.

It is in response to this situation that American churches of all denominations—and over 35,000 individual Americans who follow their own conscience—have come together to form the nationwide Sanctuary Movement.

Though based on religious principles of sanctuary, the Movement is not the property of any one religious denomination. On the contrary, like the Underground Railroad before the Civil War, the Sanctuary Movement brings together individuals of all reli-

---
A Holocaust

The sanctuary movement has wide support.
Why are thousands of religious people willing to
proclaim sanctuary and risk arrest?

There is a holocaust happening in Central
America fueled by U.S. military aid. Some 40,000
civilians have died in El Salvador, mostly at the
hands of right-wing death squads and government soldiers. Another 100,000 have been mas-
sacred in Guatemala since 1954 due to government repression.

Michael McConnell, USA Today, 1984
---

gions, as well as many whose support is based simply on American principles of justice and concern for human life and liberty.

The Christic Institute

The Christic Institute has established the Sanctuary Defense
Fund to defend in the courts those American citizens charged
with "illegally" helping these political refugees—and to keep
these helpless victims from being sent to be murdered in cold
blood.

Stacey Merkt has already been charged by the Justice Department, tried and convicted. She could be sentenced to up to 15
years in prison and fined.

But the Christic Institute has already filed an appeal to reverse
this conviction. This is a tremendously important case because it
is the first one the Government has brought against a member
of the Sanctuary Movement. This appeal will directly impact the
fate of the more than 100 sanctuaries already in existence and
the thousands of dedicated volunteer workers—as well as the
life or death of many hundreds of refugees now being sheltered
in these sanctuaries.

A victory in the higher courts could have a tremendous impact in many directions.

The Underground Railroad—an American tradition

This is not the first time there has been an Underground Railroad in America to help those fleeing from injustice. In the
years before the Civil War, thousands of free Americans, black

and white alike, organized to help runaway slaves escape to freedom. The "conductors" led slaves along the escape route where they found sanctuary in "stations"—homes, churches, farms—on their way to freedom in the U.S. or Canada. The Underground Railroad and "conductors" like Harriet Tubman and Frederick Douglass—struck a tremendous blow against slavery and for freedom. Then too, this railroad was declared illegal by the Federal Executive Dept. and those helping the slaves could be (and were) fined and imprisoned under the Fugitive Slave Act. Stacey Merkt, Jack Elder, Brother John and the many other Sanctuary workers are following in this great tradition.

THE FLIGHT FROM POVERTY

Elliott Abrams

Elliott Abrams made this statement before the House Committee on the Judiciary Subcommittee on Immigration, Refugees and International Law in his capacity as Assistant Secretary of State for Human Rights and Humanitarian Affairs under the Reagan Administration.

Points To Consider

1. Why should most Salvadoran refugees be returned to their country?
2. What is the definition of political asylum?
3. Why do some groups want all Salvadoran illegal aliens to be allowed to remain in the U.S.?
4. What is said about terror and murder faced by refugees returned to El Salvador?

Excerpted from testimony by Elliott Abrams before the House Subcommittee on Immigration, Refugees and International Law, 1984.

We have not come across a single case of abuse or murder of a deportee, nor has anyone contacted suggested that he knew of such a case.

El Salvador is a country troubled by poverty, violence, over-population, and a history of oppression. For a number of years, Salvadorans have taken advantage of economic opportunity elsewhere. Prior to the war between El Salvador and Honduras in 1969, a large number were living in Honduras. Through the 1970s, hundreds of thousands of Salvadorans came to the U.S. The increased violence in El Salvador prevalent since 1980 no doubt increased the incentives to leave the country, as have the economic difficulties which the war has only worsened.

The U.S. is thus confronted with a number of significant immigration issues regarding El Salvador. It is difficult for Salvadorans to get visitors' visas to the U.S. and difficult for them to get immigrant visas as well. We face a very significant amount of illegal immigration from El Salvador, and a large quantity of asylum applications. How do we deal with the asylum applications? To those not entitled to asylum, how do we respond to their desire to live in the United States? . . .

In fact we have no "asylum policy" toward El Salvador or any other country; we apply the same standards to each. In the last few months recommendations for the approval of applications from Salvadorans and Nicaraguans have been running at roughly the same rate, and though of course there are variations for both countries, about 15 percent of applications can meet legal standards. This reflects no policy decision, nor does it reflect the state of our bilateral relations with either government; it simply reflects the fact that asylum applicants must meet the legal standards in order to be granted asylum. We are well aware that much criticism could be ended were the number of Salvadoran asylum applications that are approved higher. But, to approve asylum applications for partisan political reasons would ignore the law. In fact, we recommended in favor of applications that meet the standards and against those that do not.

All should not remain

The argument is made that all Salvadorans, even those who do not qualify for asylum, should not be deported to El Salvador but rather allowed to remain here. As you know, the Administration does not concur with this view. All decisions require a balancing of judgments about their foreign policy, humanitarian,

103

Urban slum in El Salvador

and immigration policy implications. In the case of El Salvador, the immigration policy implications are enormous. Here we have a country with a history of large-scale illegal immigration to the U.S. An intelligent and industrious Salvadoran weighing a decision to try illegal immigration to the U.S. knows that one of the risks is deportation, which might occur before he has had a chance to earn back the costs of the journey. If we remove that possibility of deportation, it is simple logic to suggest that the illegal entry becomes a more attractive investment.

Of course, not all Salvadoran migrants to the U.S. are solely or primarily economic migrants; some are refugees who may be and have been granted asylum. (Asylum is granted to refugees fleeing persecution.) So by definition, what we are discussing is generally whether people who emigrate from El Salvador to the United States illegally should be permitted to reside here. If one says yes to this question then we do not have an immigration policy with regard to El Salvador. We have abdicated the responsibility to have one.

Persecution and death

Some groups argue that illegal aliens who are sent back to El Salvador there meet persecution and often death. Obviously, we do not believe these claims or we would not deport these people. Twice in recent years the U.S. Embassy in San Salvador has made attempts to track deportees and see if they were being persecuted; we concluded that they were not. Last summer we asked some officials of Tutela Legal, which is the human rights office of the Archdiocese of El Salvador, whether they believed there was a pattern of persecution of deportees. They replied that they did not. It is noteworthy that these accusations which are lodged by some American activist groups critical of the U.S. policy in El Salvador, find no echo nor did they find their source in complaints from Salvadoran human rights groups, which have never made this claim. And that stands to reason. El Salvador is a country, as noted above, in which emigration abroad is a common and respected means of self-improvement, and it would be odd to think that this action engaged in by hundreds and thousands of Salvadorans, by perhaps a quarter of the population, was viewed by anyone as proof of communist association. I submit that the notion that the people being deported are easily identifiable when they return to El Salvador is false, and the notion that they are automatically suspect is equally false . . .

What is remarkable is that we have not come across a single case of abuse or murder of a deportee, nor has anyone contacted suggested that he knew of such a case. I would not sug-

Economic Migrants

Judging from recent experience, most Salvadorans in the United States are not refugees fleeing persecution but would-be immigrants who want to live here. Indeed, 10 years ago, well before the Salvadoran insurgency began, a quarter of a million to a half a million Salvadorans were estimated to be in this country illegally. Their presence reflects a long-standing pattern of economic migration to the United States stemming from the fact that El Salvador, besides being poor, is the most densely populated country in the Western Hemisphere . . .

Moreover, when human rights or church groups call all Salvadorans "refugees," regardless of the facts of their individual cases, they blur the vital distinction between economic migrants and genuine refugees.

Elliott Abrams, New York Times, *1984*

gest to this Subcommittee that we have completed here the definitive scientific study and that no further efforts are needed, and indeed our own efforts are continuing. But surely there must come a time when any fair-minded observer concludes that this alleged pattern of wide-scale abuse of deportees is just a fiction unsupported by evidence.

I am sometimes asked why the U.S. does not do anything to solve the humanitarian problem of poverty and displaced persons and violence in El Salvador. This is a startling question, when you consider the enormous amount of American diplomatic and political effort aimed at bringing democracy and peace to El Salvador, and the extraordinary amounts of economic aid which we give and increased amounts which the Administration has urged upon Congress.

EXAMINING COUNTERPOINTS

This activity may be used as an individualized study guide for students in libraries and resource centers or as a discussion catalyst in small group and classroom discussions.

The Point
El Salvador is now a democracy. There is a free press, elections are held and rival politicians denounce each other in giant public rallies.

The Counterpoint
El Salvador is a brutal right-wing military dictatorship that has tortured and murdered over 40,000 of its own people.

● ● ● ●

The Point
The killings on the left in El Salvador are more numerous than the killings on the right.

The Counterpoint
The killings on the right in El Salvador are more numerous than the killings on the left.

● ● ● ●

The Point
Most refugees flee from Central America for economic reasons and should not be given sanctuary in the U.S.

The Counterpoint
Most refugees flee from Central America because of political terror and should be given sanctuary in the U.S.

● ● ● ●

The Point
The U.S. must send military aid to El Salvador. There is no need for U.S. soldiers in the region as local citizens will fight for their freedom. The leftist guerrillas continue to kill, terrorize and intimidate the local population. Bridges are blown up, roads are destroyed and public facilities are attacked.

The Counterpoint
The U.S. should stop all military aid to El Salvador. Each dawn mutilated bodies of civilians appear in ditches to remind the poor of the barbaric system under which they live—under the jackboot of the Salvadoran military. No wonder the revolutionaries move among the people like fish through the sea.

Guidelines

Part A
Examine the counterpoints above and then consider the following questions.

1. Do you agree more with the point or counterpoint in each case? Why?

2. Which reading in this publication best illustrates the point in each case?

3. Which reading best illustrates each counterpoint?

4. Do any cartoons in this publication illustrate the meaning of the point or counterpoint arguments? Which ones and why?

Part B
Social issues are usually complex, but often problems become oversimplified in political debates and discussions. Usually a polarized version of social conflict does not adequately represent the diversity of views that surround social conflict. Examine the counterpoints above. Then write down other possible interpretations of events in Central America.

CHAPTER 5

GLOBAL PERSPECTIVES: THE CONFLICT IN CENTRAL AMERICA

READINGS

U.S. TERRORISM IN CENTRAL AMERICA

The German Democratic Republic

The following statement was reprinted from **Panorama DDR,** *an official publication of the German Democratic Republic (East Germany). It was issued through the information office of the German Democratic Republic in Washington, D.C.*

Points To Consider

1. How is U.S. policy described?
2. What examples of U.S. policy are discussed?
3. What is meant by the term "reactionary regimes?"
4. Why do they believe the U.S. supports reactionary regimes?

Excerpted from a position paper by the German Democratic Republic, issued to the publisher in March of 1984.

There are many incidents which prove that the appropriate institutions in the USA are preaching and practicing a policy towards the Latin American states and peoples which relies on methods like intimidation, interference, blackmail and terrorism—brutally and blatantly, in the style of a colonial power. The threats and provocations which have been snowballing ever since Reagan took office are aimed against socialist Cuba, the people's revolutions in Nicaragua and Grenada, the popular struggle in El Salvador, Guatemala and many other countries on the subcontinent. At the same time this policy is designed to use every possible means to prop up dictatorships—whether in Chile, Paraguay, Haiti or anywhere else. And any governments or social forces which fail to bow in silence to Washington's wishes also become targets . . .

The Monroe doctrine

It was under the banner of the Monroe doctrine that the subcontinent became a "back yard" for the USA, and the "poorhouse" of America. Around the turn of the century the situation seemed safe enough to shift over to the politics of the big stick. Theodore Roosevelt, commander of a voluntary regiment in the Spanish-American War and President of the USA from 1901 to 1909, introduced the motto: Speak softly and carry a big stick!

112

A whole army of ideologues ostentatiously justified the "drive towards the south" which was growing stronger in the USA. A clear example is N. Spykman, who argued that U.S. power undoubtedly placed it in a position of hegemony over the greater part of the New World. "We," he observed, "are far stronger than our neighbours in the north and in the south." The U.S. ruled completely over Central America and was capable of exerting effective pressure on the northern part of South America. (Cf. *United States and the Balance of Power*, New York, 1942, p. 89).

U.S. General Smedley Butler is more specific in his memoirs. He describes how, in 1914, he helped to secure Mexico, and Tampico in particular, for "American" oil interests, and how he helped "civilize" Haiti and Cuba so that the National City Bank could collect its revenue there. From 1909 to 1912, he continues, he helped clean up Nicaragua for an international banking house, and in 1916 he brought "light to the darkness of the Dominican Republic" in the interests of the American sugar trade. In 1905, he adds, he tidied up Honduras for "American" banana companies.

History is extremely informative when it comes to observing the means used by the United States over the decades to "tidy up" political developments over and over again in Latin American countries. Here are some notable examples:

● **1846–1848:** Mexico, the only Latin American country to share a border with the USA, lost almost half its territory to the United States after a war of plunder.

● **1898:** The United States robbed Cuba of its tangible victory in the War of Independence against Spanish colonialism; the island won nominal independence, but the U.S. set up a naval base in the Bay of Guantánamo, which it still maintains today, and also inserted an additional article into the Constitution granting itself the "right" to occupy the republic militarily any time it chose. Until the Batista regime was brought down in 1959 it made use of this on a number of occasions when it felt its interests were in jeopardy.

● In the early decades of this century there was hardly a single country in central America or the Caribbean which was spared U.S. intervention or punitive military expeditions.

● **1954:** The United Fruit Company got the professional troops in Honduras, who had been trained by the CIA and equipped by the U.S. to march into Guatemala and overthrow the legitimate Arbenz government.

● **1961:** Heavily armed counter-revolutionaries and mercenaries trained and briefed by the CIA landed in Playa Girón (Bay of Pigs). The intervention squad was eliminated by socialist Cuba in less than three days.

- **1965:** The CIA staged a military intervention by the U.S.A. in the Dominican Republic.
- **1973:** The legitimate Popular Unity government in Chile, led by President Salvador Allende, was toppled with the considerable involvement of the Pentagon, the U.S. State Department, the CIA and U.S. monopolies.
- **Today:** It is only with all-embracing support from the U.S.A. that the brutal, repressive regime in El Salvador is clinging to power; the tiny land has become a hive of activity for U.S. military advisers and CIA agents.

The Uruguayan writer Eduardo Galeano recently portrayed this attitude in sarcastic terms:

"The history of North American interventions in Central America and the Caribbean and in the rest of Latin America—a history of unabated dirtiness and cruelty—has proceeded shoulder to shoulder with the emergence and consolidation of the United States as a world power . . .

Open complicity with reactionary regimes

The most elementary human rights are brutally repressed, terror rules unbridled and living standards are at rock bottom in those countries where the United States is hardest at work propping up their regimes from all sides . . .

The following examples illustrate how far the U.S.A. is prepared to go in continuing to support certain regimes, even when these have been discredited throughout the world, and how disastrous U.S. policy is for the peoples concerned. These examples also show how generously the state money flows in for economic and military help, which is usually presented as "an aid to security". The banks and monopolies also have their fingers in this pie, shoring up regimes hostile to the people with investments and loans.

Example Chile:

- There are four U.S. companies amongst the ten banks which are doing the most to support the Pinochet regime (Bank of America, Chase Manhattan, Morgan Guaranty, American Express). In 1979/80 alone, U.S. banks put up 354.31 million dollars for the fascist junta.
- The country is becoming increasingly dependent on international monopolies such as ITT, Anaconda, Kennecott, Exxon and General Motors.
- Even though Chile has been under a state of emergency for over eight years, with 30,000 or more Chileans brutally murdered, another 2,500 "disappeared" without trace, the U.S.

114

Administration insists that the Pinochet regime has made "progress in the direction of human rights". The "reward" consists of state credits from Washington . . .

Example El Salvador:

● "Security aid" for the reactionary regime in El Salvador has been rising especially steeply over recent years . . .
● The more money Washington pays, the more people are murdered. Since October 1979 when the junta took power, some 30,000 of the little country's 4,500,000 inhabitants have fallen prey to the systematic exterminations.

Example Guatemala:

● For the last 15 years there has been one political murder every five hours in Guatemala. They say there are almost no political prisoners in the country, since only a privilege or an accident

---

The American Death Squads

As any sophisticated politician knows, death squads have been an important part of American foreign policy for many years. Some people forget that the U.S. set up official death squads in Vietnam, to point out alleged National Liberation Front (NLF) sympathizers who were to be killed. Of course, many innocent Vietnamese were then murdered . . .

Death squads are as American as apple pie. According to columnist Jack Anderson (1/24/84), the first death squad was established in Guatemala by the CIA as it worked to overthrow president Jacobo Arbenz, in 1954. Since then, the agency has set up and trained death squads in many nations, from Latin America to the notorious SAVAK which operated under the Shah. To quote Anderson, "The CIA has continued to maintain contacts inside the death squads." To all intents and purposes, the death squads in El Salvador are merely an extension of the CIA.

David A. Michaels, Daily World, *1984*

can bring you still living before a judge. 70,000 Guatemalans have been killed since the military putsch in 1954, and 50,000 internally deported for political reasons . . .

• According to the magazine **Informador Guillero**, the U.S.A. has provided Guatemala with 50 million dollars just to fight the liberation movement there. Jeremiah O'Leary, a U.S. security specialist coordinating the effective use of military aid against the liberation movement with the Guatemalan government, recently visited the country.

• 77 big U.S. companies are taking their pickings from the plundering of Guatemala's wealth. While the junta's army is reckoned to be the best trained and equipped in central America thanks to cooperation with the United States, "70 per cent of Guatemalans . . . have to live on an annual income of 120 marks. Only 12 per cent of the population can reap the benefits of social insurance . . ."

The repressive dictatorships in Central America and the Caribbean would not last a week if they did not receive unconditional support from the U.S.A. The most aggressive elements in the U.S. Administration have recently been making it increasingly clear that they would not flinch from direct military intervention if their puppet regimes were threatened with collapse and "U.S. interests" were seen to be in jeopardy.

Washington indicted from all quarters

It is always the same. Be it the Middle East or southern Africa, south-east Asia, Central America or the Caribbean—anywhere on this planet where hotbeds of conflict arise, the most aggressive elements of United States society are actively and decisively involved. They support the most reactionary regimes, who are absolutely dependent on this back-up to engage in their repeated acts of aggression–Israel in Lebanon, the South African apartheid regime against neighbouring states, and the brutal regimes in El Salvador, Chile, Guatemala and elsewhere against their own people. The terrorism exported by the U.S.A., in all its many guises, has become the scourge of humanity.

DEMOCRATIC VALUES IN CENTRAL AMERICA

The Norwegian Embassy

This article was reprinted from a speech by Mr. Svenn Stray before the Parliament of Norway. Svenn Stray is the Norwegian Foreign Minister and made this speech to outline his government's basic attitude toward social change and revolution in Central America.

Points To Consider

1. What are social conditions like in Central America?
2. What is the Sandinista Government and what promise has it failed to keep?
3. How is the Contadora Group described and what is its role?
4. How is Norway's policy toward Central America defined?

Excerpted from a speech by Foreign Minister Svenn Stray made before the Parliament of Norway on March 7, 1984.

At the root of Central America's conflicts are economic and social problems, which cannot be solved by military means.

The situation in Central America is marked by an extensive guerrilla campaign, acts of violence and violations of human rights. These conditions are exacerbated by the fact that Nicaragua and El Salvador in particular are subject to outside interference and receive substantial military aid from countries outside the region . . .

Nicaraguan revolution

Nearly five years after the revolution in Nicaragua, the Sandinista government has yet to keep its original promises to create a non-aligned pluralist society with a mixed economy. On the contrary, the trend has been towards a totalitarian system. The announcement of elections to be held for president, vice president, and legislative assembly is a sign that conditions in the country may develop in a democratic direction. If the elections are held in accordance with normal democratic principles, this will give the government a legitimacy which is also very likely to have a considerable impact on the country's relations with other states.

Contadora group

Hope that the conflicts in the region may be resolved attaches first and foremost to the peace plan agreed on by the Contadora group and the five Central American countries concerned. The most important proposals contained in the plan call for control of and limitations on military forces in the countries in question, a timetable for the withdrawal of foreign military advisers, the elimination of destabilizing revolutionary groups and the support they receive from outside, a timetable for holding free elections, respect for human rights, and economic and social measures.

Economic and social problems

At the root of Central America's conflicts are economic and social problems, which cannot be solved by military means. Any solution will have to be based on democratic values and respect for human rights. A more just distribution of the benefits of society, the principles of non-interference and respect for national integrity. These objectives are also fundamental to the efforts of the Contadora group. Norway has therefore consistently sup-

118

NICARAGUA

Vital Statistics

Area: 57,145 square miles (about the size of Iowa)
Population: 2.5 million (slightly larger than the Mpls.-St. Paul area)
Life Expectancy: 52 Years
Annual Per Capita Income: $600
Bordering Countries: Honduras and Costa Rica

ported the group's work and expressed the hope that the peace plan will lead to results.

The U.S.A. has given its support in principle to the Contadora group's peace plan. At the same time there is reason to point

Outside intervention

"... We are following with concern developments in Central America, where in El Salvador, but also elsewhere, the use of force and bloodshed are on the increase.

The peoples of that region must be enabled to determine their own destiny free from direct or indirect intervention from outside.

All democratic forces in these countries should act in awareness of their common responsibility and dissociate themselves from the forces of violence.

Federal Republic of Germany Ambassador Hans-Dietrich Genscher, 1981

out that the United States Congress has had submitted to it a bill which is based on the Kissinger commission's analyses and recommendations concerning the future United States role in Central America. The bill aims at promoting the right to self-determination, economic and social development, respect for human rights, and cooperation to meet threats to security in the region. The realization of this part of the bill will be an important contribution to the realization of the Contadora group's peace plan for the region.

Military aid

In addition the bill contains proposals for military assistance for the next few years amounting to 580 million dollars, in the main earmarked for El Salvador and Honduras. To give military assistance to such an extent seems to conflict with an important element in the peace plan relating to limitations in armed forces. However, the U.S.A. explains that such aid is necessary as long as the insurgent groups also receive military assistance from outside.

In the last few years, Norway has strengthened contacts with Nicaragua and Costa Rica. The humanitarian and economic aid which Norway has provided for the region is meant as a contribution to social and economic development and confidence in our country has been strengthened by this. There is a broad measure of support for continuing these endeavors.

120

19

GLOBAL PERSPECTIVES

AMERICAN AGGRESSION IN EL SALVADOR

The Cuban Newspaper, **Granma**

This article was excerpted from an editorial by Alexis Shelton in Granma. *Alexis Shelton is on the international staff of* Granma, *the official paper and publication of the Cuban Revolution and Fidel Castro's revolutionary government. Alexis Shelton describes how the revolutionary forces in El Salvador are responding to U.S. intervention.*

Points To Consider

1. What is the FMLN?
2. How extensive is the control of the FMLN?
3. Why have the guerrillas been effective?
4. What is happening to the Salvadoran army?

Alexis Shelton, "A War Whose Strategic Initiative is of the People," *Granma,* January 29, 1984.

121

A day must come when the United States, prompted by the sheer force of the events, will have to accept that the historical reality of the Central American peoples is indissolubly tied to freedom and independence.

Retaking the strategic initiative in the war was the Salvadoran people's main goal. The U.S. administration was forced to enmesh itself deeper and deeper in the conflict, thus clearly revealing its aggressive and interventionist stand . . .

The most important guerrilla operations last year took place in the departments of San Vicente and Usulután. Generally speaking, the Farabundo Martí National Liberation Front (FMLN) virtually controls the eastern part of the country. The FMLN is now strategically superior in eight of the country's 14 departments, namely: Chalatenango and Morazán, where it holds nearly total control; Cabañas and Cuscatlán, zones of expansion and consolidation; San Vicente, San Miguel, La Unión and Usulután, zones now under dispute and subject to growing military operations.

Thanks to their persistent strategy of prolonged warfare, the rebels have been able to neutralize the growing presence of U.S. advisers and a stepped-up supply of arms and war matériel going to the demoralized Salvadoran army.

Military balance

Politically speaking, the planned elections imposed by Washington on the Salvadoran regime are still being developed in spite of the fact that not even minimum conditions exist which would enable most people to go to the polls and cast their ballots. The regime is merely trying to implement a formula whereby it can introduce some reforms to mask its scorched-earth war. The United States is bent on improving the image of the Salvadoran regime.

Thoroughly familiar with the terrain and supported by broad sectors of the population, the guerrillas have been able to deal repeated blows to the army and make quick moves in many places. Guerrilla control over the country's leading roads and neighboring areas has played a fundamental role in this.

During the "Against Aggression, El Salvador Will Win" campaign, which was launched on May 25, 1983, the enemy took a severe beating. Then the "Independence, Freedom and Democracy for El Salvador" campaign began with the attack on the San Miguel Garrison where the 3rd army infantry brigade was sta-

122

"The CIA guys say the sister of the island's Prime Minister studied ballet at the Bolshoi!"

tioned, plus sabotage, harassment and the destruction of lesser targets in the same department of San Miguel.

During the latter campaign, the FMLN mobilized some 7000 fighters and organized them into battalions, detachments and brigades resembling a regular army structure combined with the flexibility inherent to guerrilla warfare. For approximately two months the insurgents attacked over 60 towns in nine departments and inflicted around 800 casualties on the armed forces.

CIA Organized Death Squads

● Contrary to Reagan's claims that the "small, violent right wing" in El Salvador "are not a part of the government," and that they have "consistently" been opposed by the U.S., the death squads were organized by the CIA starting in 1963, and many Salvadoran officials, most notably Colonel Nicholas Carranza, director of the Treasury Police, have long been on the CIA payroll. Reagan talks piously about the terrible Sandinistas "publicly humiliating Catholic priests." He neglects to mention that it was the U.S.-organized death squads that assassinated Salvadoran Archbishop Oscar Romero after a public warning from Roberto D'Aubuisson, leader of El Salvador's Constituent Assembly.

The United States' role in establishing the death squads is well documented in an important article by Allen Nairn in the May issue of *The Progressive* that has been ignored by most of the media.

In These Times *Editorial, 1984*

On December 14, 1983, the balance of military forces experienced a spectacular twist when the FMLN captured the strategic Cacahuatique Hill in Morazan department and took prisoner the command officers of an army unit. In that action the regime troops sustained 144 casualties: 60 dead, 75 wounded and nine prisoners.

The capture of the hill involved taking over the largest army communications base in the eastern part of the country, plus the command post of a counterinsurgency operation employing over 3000 troops.

Two surprise attacks opened the guerrilla offensive this year which shook the regime's military structure at a time when it was trying to regain the war initiative.

On December 30, FMLN vanguard units captured El Paraíso military base in Chalatenango, where the 4th special troops brigade, considered the country's top military brigade, was deployed. In that action the guerrillas caused the army 300 casualties.

Two days later, on January 1, 1984, the rebels destroyed the Cuscatlán Bridge, 95 kilometers from San Salvador, which had been the largest one still intact after the destruction of De Oro Bridge in 1981. The bridge was protected by 200 soldiers.

New organization

The way most recent military campaigns have evolved points to the substantial qualitative changes in the new organizational and operational scheme that provides greater ability for mobilizing and concentrating rebel troops, improved firepower and logistics and, especially, a far better coordination of forces.

The training of FMLN troops on the basis of a common organizational plan represents a starting point for structuring a national people's army which features a joint general headquarters and individual command arrangements at every level.

While the guerrillas are making overall advances everywhere, the Salvadoran army is degenerating and becoming less and less capable in its response. It is also negatively affected by the upheaval caused to the strategic war scheme designed and sponsored by the "all-powerful" U.S. advisers.

No doubt the U.S. is faced with the inevitable task of again readjusting its planned politico-military goals for El Salvador given that the existing scheme is now at a crossroad that points to an uncontainable crisis. Notwithstanding the optimism with which the Pentagon conceived these goals, the pressure exerted by the guerrillas has proved just too strong.

The tenacity and heroism with which the Salvadorans are waging their struggle on the war fronts indicate that a day must come when the United States, prompted by the sheer force of the events, will have to accept that the historical reality of the Central American peoples is indissolubly tied to freedom and independence.

NEGOTIATIONS, NOT INTERVENTION

The French Information Service

This article was reprinted from a speech by Claude Cheysson, the Minister of External Relations for the government of France. The speech was made to the French National Assembly in response to a member's question on the issue of conflict in Central America. Claude Cheysson describes the basic policy of France toward Central America in this speech.

Points To Consider

1. What is the policy of France toward Central America?
2. How is military action in Central America described?
3. Why does France favor the Contadora Group approach?
4. How is the situation in El Salvador described?

Excerpted from a speech by Claude Cheysson, Minister of External Relations, to the French National Assembly, November 23, 1983.

The outlook will be disastrous unless political dialogue is started between all the political forces in El Salvador—those of the Junta, and also the liberation fronts.

The French government is concerned about the situation in Central America.

The underlying causes of the situation have been described by President Mitterrand repeatedly since his speech in Mexico.

There is the injustice that has reigned in these countries, a legacy of the colonial period. There is a systematic game being played by foreign forces keeping alive the tensions which unfortunately exist in this part of the world.

What is the answer to all this?
France believes that there, as elsewhere, the countries of the region should take their destiny into their own hands and that they should make every effort to deal with the problems that concern them. For this reason we have supported the efforts of the Contadora Group ever since it was instituted. The other European countries have made statements along these lines as well.

When the Contadora Group succeeded in Cancun on July 17 in formulating a plan for Central America, it is remarkable that not a single country in the world opposed it: not the United States, nor Cuba, nor the Soviet Union, nor the Europeans, nor the Latin American countries. No country had anything but praise for the plan.

The discussions that followed were difficult. Meetings took place between the four countries of the Contadora Group and the five countries of Central America. Finally, a statement of goals was formulated in Panama two months ago and this has provided, in our view, the basis for a settlement.

Progress has been achieved since then. The Nicaraguans presented in their turn a draft proposal which conforms largely to the statement of goals of the Contadora Group. The Organization of American States has supported the project. We support its initiatives in every possible way.

This, and not military maneuvers, is the way to make progress, I believe.

As I said when I was in the region, I do not see how an aircraft carrier, ten aircraft carriers, one thousand, ten thousand or fifty thousand men will speed up the implementation of the Contadora proposals. I do see clearly, however, how direct contact among these countries would allow them to find a more harmonious solution.

El Salvador

This should certainly have an effect on the situation in El Salvador. There, as elsewhere, dialogue between the political forces is the way to deal with tensions, not a military build-up which is singularly ineffective.

The pace in El Salvador has speeded up again. We face frightening statistics today. It is not a question of 200 dead or missing in a few months, but of 30 to 40 dead or missing per week. The recent mission by Henry Kissinger has improved nothing.

The outlook will be disastrous unless political dialogue is started between all the political forces in El Salvador—those of the Junta, and also the liberation fronts. We shall continue to work to this end and we will certainly encourage the few slightly more promising signs that have emerged recently.

This way, in this region and elsewhere, we believe we can serve the cause of human rights and the right of peoples through which men express themselves collectively.

It is my conviction that many of the revolutions and wars in the third world are rooted first of all in the soil of poverty and in the economic exploitation that exacerbate the traditional confrontations between ethnic groups, religions and parties.

Civil wars are not triggered by external influences alone, even if they may serve foreign interests. Their roots lie deep in the legacy of the past. Thus the peoples of Central America have a long history marked by military oppression, social inequality and the confiscation of economic resources and political power by a few. Today each of them must be allowed to find its own path toward greater justice, greater democracy and greater independence and must be allowed to do so without interference or manipulation. My country has in the past encouraged sincere action aimed at finding a peaceful solution to conflicts and refusing recourse to force between neighboring countries, and it will continue to do so in the future.

But let us understand that before calm can return we must first reduce the level of misery in the world. It serves no purpose to hammer away at building peace while we allow the underlying and permanent causes of war to prosper.

This is why developing a shared prosperity is an urgent priority .

MEXICAN POLICY IN CENTRAL AMERICA

Walter Astié Burgos

Walter Astié Burgos is a minister for the Mexican Government. He made these comments in the United States before the Close Up Foundation, Washington, D.C. He relates Mexico's attitude toward the conflict in Central America, military intervention in the region and the path to peaceful resolution of social and economic problems.

Points To Consider

1. How is the basic social and economic conflict described?
2. Why and how has Mexico attempted to encourage reconciliation?
3. What specific commitments does the Contadora Group want the nations of Central America to work toward?
4. What will military force accomplish?

Excerpted from a speech by Minister Walter Astié Burgos to the Close Up Foundation in Washington, D.C., February 23, 1984.

The absence of dialogue and negotiations seriously endangered the peace and security of Central America and so far the formula of the Contadora group is the only alternative to the military solution.

In what concerns our foreign policy, I want, first of all, to mention that "the basic principles of the philosophy of Mexican foreign policy, are the result of historical experience and more precisely, the result of Mexico's struggle to maintain its independence. The independence from Spain, the war with the United States, the French Invasion and other conflicts and pressures which Mexico endured throughout the 19th and early 20th centuries, all set the stage for the elaboration of a doctrine which is based on the principles of: respect for national sovereignty and freedom, self-determination, non-intervention in the domestic affairs of states, respect and compliance with treaties and international law, the peaceful settlement of conflicts, and international cooperation.

"Mexico has to its credit the fact that it has never started a war, nor has it ever initiated an armed attack against any other country. The observance of international law and the use of diplomatic as well as political negotiations, are the most appropriate measures in order to avoid war."

From the onset of the Central American crisis, we recognize that its causes are rooted in the economic deficiencies, the lack of social and political freedom, the need to update structures towards a greater political and economic democracy, and the absence of respect of the human rights."

The basic conflict

Summarizing, we consider the main problem to be the need to promote economic and social development. The clash between the privileged and the destitute, has given rise to armed confrontation which, far from promoting economic development, destroys the limited possibilities available for the improvement of the standards of living of the majority of the population. That is what happened in Nicaragua, is taking place in El Salvador, and could spread to Honduras and Guatemala. For this reason, it is our opinion that an authentic effort on the part of the Central American countries, as well as of other nations with interest in the region, such as the United States of America, Mexico, Venezuela, and Colombia, is needed in order to promote economic

130

development as the main instrument to arrest armed confrontation.

Considering the current existence of a belligerent movement, Mexico has attempted to encourage reconciliation of the contending parties as the first step necessary to attain stability. In the case of El Salvador, the governments of France and Mexico made a joint statement stressing their belief that the only possible way to put a halt to the civil war in that country, was through dialogue and negotiation. Therefore, it was necessary to recognize the guerrilla movement as a political force; consequently it should be taken into consideration in any negotiations geared to a solution of the crisis in the country, as in any other step towards democratic elections.

In the same manner, and while being aware of the existence of a number of complex factors affecting the stability of Central America, Mexico has emphasized since the beginning of the crisis, the need to approach the three main centers of tension: thus, we proposed:
1. Dialogue between Washington and Havana.
2. Dialogue between the "guerrilla" and the government of El Salvador.
3. Dialogue between Nicaragua and Honduras.

In 1982, and with the aim of reducing the possibility of war between Nicaragua and Honduras—which still continues to exist—the presidents of Venezuela and Mexico proposed a meeting of the leaders of Honduras and Nicaragua. For this purpose the presidents requested the support of other Central and Latin American countries and that of the United States. Though said meeting never took place, the initiative somehow helped to reduce the risks of armed confrontation in that moment.

Contadora group

The diplomatic endeavor of Mexico, essentially directed to promote negotiation, has continued through the mechanism known as the "Contadora Group" which is integrated by Colombia, Mexico, Panama, and Venezuela. The main objective of the group is to reach a common understanding, by means of a dialogue . . .

The Contadora group wishes to create, through negotiations, a wide framework that could be acceptable and useful by all the parties involved, a framework that is based on the democratic principles of dialogue, negotiation, tolerance and plurality, that are the basis of our internal political systems and must be also the guidelines for our foreign policy.

WHAT IS POLITICAL BIAS?

This activity may be used an an individualized study guide for students in libraries and resource centers or as a discussion catalyst in small group and classroom discussions.

Many readers are unaware that written material usually expresses an opinion or bias. The skill to read with insight and understanding requires the ability to detect different kinds of bias. Political bias, race bias, sex bias, ethnocentric bias and religious bias are five basic kinds of opinions expressed in editorials and literature that attempt to persuade. This activity will focus on political bias defined in the glossary below.

FIVE KINDS OF EDITORIAL OPINION OR BIAS

*sex bias—the expression of dislike for and/or feeling of superiority over a person because of gender or sexual preference

*race bias—the expression of dislike for and/or feeling of superiority over a racial group

*ethnocentric bias—the expression of a belief that one's own group, race, religion, culture or nation is superior. Ethnocentric persons judge others by their own standards and values

*political bias—the expression of opinions and attitudes about government related issues on the local, state or international level

*religious bias—the expression of a religious belief or attitude

Guidelines

Read through the following statements and decide which ones represent political opinions or bias. Evaluate each statement by using the method indicated.

Place the letter (P) in front of any sentence that reflects political opinion or bias. Place the letter (N) in front of any sentence that does not reflect political opinion or bias. Place the letter (S) in front of any sentence that you are not sure about.

132

___ 1. Political violence in Central America is largely a result of Soviet and Cuban intervention.

___ 2. The United States military and CIA have been secretly aiding right-wing death squads in Central America.

___ 3. Civil War in Central America is caused by widespread poverty and political oppression.

___ 4. Right-wing Salvadoran death squads assassinated Archbishop Oscar Romero.

___ 5. The United States is supporting right-wing military dictatorships in El Salvador and Guatemala.

___ 6. The United States must help El Salvador eradicate the guerrillas in El Salvador and Guatemala.

___ 7. Americans should support revolutionary change in developing nations.

___ 8. The most elementary human rights are brutally repressed and terror rules in nations where the U.S. is supporting military dictatorships.

___ 9. Left-wing terrorists kill soldiers, civilians and many other innocent people in their quest for political power.

___ 10. Right-wing death squads and the Salvadoran military have killed over 30,000 Salvadorans.

___ 11. Most refugees from Central America are trying to escape poverty.

___ 12. Refugees are fleeing violence and political terror in El Salvador.

___ 13. Military aid to El Salvador should be stopped until human rights violations are curtailed.

Other Activities

1. Locate three examples of political opinion or bias in the readings from chapter five.

2. Make up one statement that would be an example of each of the following: **sex bias, race bias, ethnocentric bias,** and **religious bias.**

3. See if you can locate any factual statements in the thirteen items listed above.

BIBLIOGRAPHY

OVERVIEW

America's Watch Report: Guatemala: A Nation of Prisoners. 36 West 44th Street, New York, NY 10036.

Amnesty International. **Political Killings by Governments** (London: Amnesty International Publications, 1983).

Arnson, Cynthia. El Salvador—A Revolution Confronts the United States. (Washington: Institute for Policy Studies, 1982). 122 pp.

Central America: International Dimensions of the Crisis. Edited by Richard E. Feinberg. (New York: Holmes & Meier, 1982). 300 pp.

Changing Course: Blueprint for Peace in Central America and the Caribbean (Washington, DC: Institute for Policy Studies, 1984).

Didion, Joan. **Salvador** (New York: Simon and Schuster, 1984).

El Salvador. **Foreign Policy,** no. 43 (Summer 1981) pp. 71–103.
    Contents.—"El Salvador: the current danger," by L. Gomez and B. Cameron.—"Choosing to Win," by W. Thompson.—A View from the Church," by J. Hebir.—"Mexico's Position," by O. Pellicer.

El Salvador: Central America in the New Cold War. Edited by Marvin E. Gettleman. (New York: Grove Press, 1981). 397 pp.

Harris, Kevin, and Mario Espinosa. "Reform, Repression, and Revolution in El Salvador." **Fletcher Forum,** v. 5 (Summer 1981) pp. 295–319.

Kruger, Alexander. **El Salvador's Marxist Revolution.** (Washington: Heritage Foundation, 1981) 14, A2 p. [Backgrounder no. 137].

LeoGrande, William M. "A Splendid Little War." **International Security,** v. 6 (Summer 1981) pp. 27–52.

McColm, R. Bruce. **El Salvador: Peaceful Revolution or Armed Struggle?** (New York: Freedom House, 1982) 47 p. (Perspectives on Freedom, no. 1).

Montgomery, Tommie Sue. **Revolution in El Salvador—Origins and Evolution.** (Boulder, Colo.: Westview Press, 1982) 255 pp.

Singer, Max. "Can El Salvador be saved?" **Commentary,** v. 72 (Dec. 1981) pp. 31–36.

Political Conditions in El Salvador

Anderson, Thomas P. **Politics in Central America: Guatemala, El Salvador, Honduras, and Nicaragua.** (New York: Praeger, 1982) 240 pp.

Gayner, Jeffrey B., and Richard Araujo. El Salvador After the Elections (Washington: Heritage Foundation, 1982) 10 pp. [Backgrounder no. 173].

Prosterman, Roy L. "The Unmaking of a Land Reform." **New Republic,** v. 187 (Aug. 9, 1982) pp. 21–25.

Report on Human Rights in El Salvador; A Report to the Board of the American Civil Liberties Union, January 1982 (Washington: Center for National Security Studies, 1982) 280 pp.

Report of the President's National Bipartisan Commission on Central America (January, 1984).

U.S. Dept. of State. El Salvador. In its Country reports on human rights practices for 1982; report submitted to the Committee on Foreign Relations, U.S. Senate, and Committee on Foreign Affairs, U.S. House of Representatives, by the Department of State.

U.S. Policies Toward El Salvador in an International Context

Araujo, Richard. Congress and Aid to El Salvador (Washington: Heritage Foundation, 1982) 14, A2 p. [Backgrounder no. 173].

Fisher, Stewart W. "Human Rights in El Salvador and U.S. Foreign Policy." **Human Rights Quarterly,** v. 4 (Spring 1982) p. 1–38.

Horton, Scott, and Randy Sellier. "The Utility of Presidential Certifications of Compliance with United States Human Rights Policy: The case of El Salvador. **Wisconsin Law Review,** v. 1982, no. 5 (1982) pp. 825–861.

Keller, Bill. "Interest Groups Focus on El Salvador Policy." **Congressional Quarterly Weekly Report,** v. 40 (Apr. 24, 1982) pp. 895-900.

"New Aid to El Salvador." **Freedom at Issue,** no. 68 (Sept.–Oct. 1982) pp. 6–12.

Pastor, Robert A. "The Target and the Source: El Salvador and Nicaragua." **Washington Quarterly,** v. 5 (Summer 1982) pp. 116–127.

"A Plan to Win in El Salvador." **Newsweek,** v. 101 (Mar. 21, 1983) pp. 18–20.

Sigmund, Paul E. "Latin America: Change or Continuity?" **Foreign Affairs,** v. 60, no. 3 (1982) pp. 629–657.

Storrs, K. Larry. Congress and El Salvador. In U.S. Library of Congress. Foreign Affairs and National Defense Division. Congress and Foreign Policy—1981 (Washington: U.S. Govt. Print. Off., 1982) pp. 115–132.

U.S. Congress. House. Committee on Appropriations. Subcommittee on Foreign Operations and Related Agencies. Supplemental appropriations for 1982. Hearings, 97th Cong., 2d sess. (Washington: U.S. Govt. Print. Off., 1982) 339 pp.

Part 2—Security assistance; El Salvador; Caribbean Basin Initiative; Security interests in Latin America.

U.S. Congress. House. Committee on Foreign Affairs. Subcommittee on Inter-American Affairs. Presidential Certification on El Salvador. Hearings, 97th Cong., 2d sess. (Washington: U.S. Govt. Print. Off., 1982) 2 v. Hearings held Feb. 2–Aug. 17, 1982.

U.S. Congress. Senate. Committee on Foreign Relations. Certification Concerning Military Aid to El Salvador. Hearings, 97th Cong., 2d sess., on the President's January 28, 1982 certification concerning military aid to El Salvador. Feb. 8 and Mar. 11, 1982 (Washington: U.S. Govt. Print. Off., 1982) 265 pp.

—— Presidental Certifications on Conditions in El Salvador. Hearing, 97th Cong., 2d sess. Aug. 3, 1982 (Washington: U.S. Govt. Print. Off., 1982) 280 pp.

U.S. Dept. of State. Bureau of Public Affairs. Certification of Progress in El Salvador: July 27, 1982–January 21, 1983 (Washington, 1983) 4 pp. (Current policy no. 449).

—— Communist Interference in El Salvador (Washington, 1981) 8 pp. (Special report no. 80).

—— Cuba's Renewed Support for Violence in Latin America (Washington, 1981) 12 pp. (Special report no. 90).

"U.S. Policy Toward Central America." **Orbis,** v. 26 (Summer 1982) pp. 305–325.

Military Advisers and Military Involvement: Are There Parallels with Vietnam?

"El Salvador Isn't Vietnam . . . But There is a Chilling Resemblance." **Washington Post** (Mar. 11, 1983) p. A17.

"The Friendly Fire [editorial]." **New Republic,** v. 186 (Feb. 17, 1982) pp. 5–7.

"Heading for Another Vietnam?" **U.S. News & World Report,** v. 94 (Mar. 21, 1983) pp. 20–24.

"How to Help El Salvador." **New Republic,** v. 188 (Mar. 28, 1983) pp. 5–7.

Kaiser, Robert G. "El Salvador & Vietnam: Is This a Replay?" **Boston Globe,** Mar. 14, 1982: pp. A21, A24.

Kirkpatrick, Jeane J. Will El Salvador go the way of Vietnam? **Human Events,** v. 43 (Mar. 5, 1983) pp. 5, 18.

LeoGrande, William M. "Salvador's No Domino." **New York Times** (Mar. 9, 1983) p. A23.

Lewis, Anthony. It's Not Vietnam, but . . ." **New York Times** (Feb. 25, 1982) p. 31.

"Reagan Sounds the Alarm." **Newsweek,** v. 101 (Mar. 14, 1983) pp. 16–20, 22–24.

Strasser, Steven. "Teaching the ABCs of War: The American Advisers in El Salvador Struggle to Turn Raw Recruits into Soldiers." By Steven Strasser with James LeMoyne. **Newsweek,** v. 101 (Mar. 28, 1983) pp. 24–25.